The Retirement Miracle

The Retirement Miracle

PATRICK KELLY

The Retirement Miracle

Cover and Interior Design Indigo Design, Inc
www.bookcoverdesignbyindigo.com

ISBN 978 0 9833615-0-3

Printed in the USA

I shall be telling this with a sigh

Somewhere ages and ages hence:

Two roads diverged in a wood, and I –

I took the one less traveled by,

And that has made all the difference.

The Road Not Taken, Robert Frost

To my Mom and Dad
Thank you…for everything.

Contents

Acknowledgements

Writing a book feels much like I imagine a walk across America. If you focus only on your destination, the sheer magnitude of the task can overwhelm you. Paralyze you. But if you take each day, one at a time, bit by bit, not only will you eventually reach your final destination, but you will also have the privilege of reveling in the joy of each day's walk.

This is a picture of my journey.

Not only have these last few years been a surprise adventure, more significantly, I have been surrounded and blessed by incredible people, all of whom I now call friends. It's a gift. A rare and unexpected gift. Thank you!

But I do need to name a special few, without whose support I would have failed.

Laura Carlson, Queen of the Cardboard – thank you for your long days and for putting your entire heart and soul into making sure all customers receive their orders. Your faithfulness and dedication humble me.

Caryn Kelly – most fathers don't get the privilege of working with their daughter ... I am blessed. I watch in awe at your maturity and talent. I love you.

Audria Wooster at Indigo Design – your talent as a designer is a wonderful gift. Thank you for your brilliant cover and for taking this manuscript and making it art.

Greg, Nathan, and Carter – each of you have become the kind of friend every person hopes for, but few actually experience. Please know that without your friendship, encouragement, and direction, my journey would have likely ended a long time ago. I am forever in your debt.

Bill Martin - thanks for your sustaining friendship and continunig encouragement. You're a true professional and an asset to our industry.

Jim Kuhlman, my trusted confidant and brother – your friendship allows me to nullify the laws of mathematics, because with your mind, one plus one always equals five.

My dear wife, Marly – thank you for willingly bearing the brunt of my travels, for making our house a wonderful home, and for being my loving wife as well as the best editor on the planet. If I could live 100 lives, I'd choose you in every one.

Special Note to Reader

This book is *not* intended to give any tax or investment advice of any kind. Neither is it intended to make or suggest any personal recommendation as to what any individual should or shouldn't choose in regard to the most fitting and appropriate financial strategy. Each person's need and situation is as unique as his or her own fingerprint. Also, and I point this out multiple times throughout this book, while these strategies exist as of the writing of this manuscript, no one can guarantee they will exist in the future. Therefore, I encourage you to seek professional advice from a knowledgeable advisor who fully understands these concepts and can not only provide you the most up-to-date information, but can clearly outline both the benefits as well as the pitfalls of this or any other strategy you might pursue. Lastly, I urge each reader to pursue only what is in his or her unique, specific, and best interest. The intent of this book is solely to introduce some of the unique and powerful concepts and strategies that life insurance and annuities can provide if utilized to their full and proper potential. I hope you find this book to be a fun journey.

Chapter 1

It's Worse than I Thought

I will never forget May 19, 2008. That day changed everything.

I was sitting in a hotel dining room eating breakfast, getting ready to host a daylong workshop for a group of financial professionals in Raleigh, North Carolina, when I just about choked on my oatmeal. Seriously, it was all I could do to keep from blowing oats all over the nicely dressed couple sitting next to me.

The headline caught my attention; the article invoked the reaction.

I picked up the morning copy of *USA Today*, and staring at me in bold print, right there on the front page, was: ***Bill for Taxpayers Swells by Trillions.***

Stunned, I read on. Here's what it said:

> *The federal government's long-term financial obligations grew by $2.5 trillion last year, a reflection of the mushrooming cost of Medicare and Social Security benefits as more baby boomers reach retirement.*
>
> *That's double the red ink of a year earlier.*

> *Taxpayers are on the hook for a record $57.3 trillion in federal liabilities to cover the lifetime benefits of everyone eligible for Medicare, Social Security and other government programs, a USA TODAY analysis found.*
>
> *That's nearly $500,000 per household.*
>
> *When obligations of state and local governments are added, the total rises to $61.7 trillion, or $531,472 per household. That is more than four times what Americans owe in personal debt such as mortgages.*
>
> *The $2.5 trillion in federal liabilities dwarfs the $162 billion the government officially announced as last year's deficit, down from $248 billion a year earlier.*
>
> *'We're running deficits in the trillions of dollars, not the hundreds of billions of dollars we're being told,' says Sheila Weinberg, chief executive of the Institute for Truth in Accounting of Chicago.*
>
> ***The reason for the discrepancy: Accounting standards require corporations and state governments to count new financial obligations, even if the payments will be made later. The federal government doesn't follow that rule. Instead of counting lifetime benefits for programs such as Social Security, the government counts the cost of benefits for the current year.[1] [Bold print by author.]***

I was gasping for air. How could this be? I had just spent the previous decade working on my book *Tax-Free Retirement*. Reading. Researching. Writing. And never once did this fact come up. Not once. How could I have missed it?

Easy. It was information that wasn't talked about. Taboo in the circles of the political elite. These numbers were clandestine. Buried.

Do you comprehend what this article is saying? Our budget deficit for 2007 was 15 times worse than official reports. Yes, 15 times! Even the phrase "Good enough for government work" can't come close to touching this discrepancy.

Let me explain in more detail what this front-page article was telling the American public. Simply put, in 2007 the U.S. government reported our country's "official" annual deficit (the amount we spent above the income we brought in) to be $162 billion – billion with a b. However, our "real" deficit for that year was actually a mind-numbing $2.5 trillion – trillion with a t.

Why the difference? Here comes the really fun part.

The U.S. government uses a set of accounting practices different from every other entity in the country, including state governments. All other entities report debt on their balance sheet the year in which they commit to the liability, not just the year in which the money is spent. Do you see the difference? It's major.

For example, let's say in 2010, Corporation X commits to a project that is going to cost $20 million over the next five years. Even though the money isn't going to all be spent in 2010, the entire $20 million has to go on that company's balance sheet as a liability, because it is money that will be spent based on the current year's decision.

Is it any surprise that the U.S. government doesn't play by the same rules? Yeah, that was my reaction as well.

Here's how everybody's favorite uncle, Uncle Sam, handles the reporting of his debt. He (the U.S. government) only reports debt in the year that the money actually leaves the U.S. coffers, not in the year in which he commits to the liability, creating an enormous disparity. A disparity so large that, when you look at our total national debt, this reporting aberration covers up a figure that is nearly six times larger than what is currently being reported to the American public.

Here are the actual numbers. I hope you're sitting down.

As of January 2011, the "official" national debt reported by the U.S. government is $14.3 trillion. However, our "real" national debt, taking into account all of our current outstanding liabilities, stands at a whopping $76.1 trillion[2] – five and a half times larger than the number the government officially reports.

Before we go any further, I want to put into perspective just how big 1 trillion really is.

Near the end of last year, I picked up my oldest son from school. On the way home he said, "Dad, do you want to know how big a trillion is?"

"Yeah," I said enthusiastically.

"Okay, guess what year it was 1 trillion seconds ago?"

"I have no idea. What year was it?"

"C'mon, Dad, you gotta guess."

"Uh … 1400?" I answered a bit pathetically.

"Nope! Not even close! It was 30,000 B.C."

"What? No way!" I said, as I tried to keep my car on the road. "That's impossible."

"Nope. Trust me. It's right. We did the math in class today."

"That can't be. That seems *way* too big," I said, wishing I could pull out a calculator right at that very moment.

And that's exactly what I did when I got home. And he was right.

Let me walk you through the simple math I performed to verify that answer.

Seconds per Day = 86,400 (24 hours X 60 minutes X 60 seconds)

Seconds per Year = 31,536,000 (86,400 seconds per day X 365 days)

Number of Years in 1 Trillion Seconds=31,710 (1,000,000,000,000 / 31,536,000)

Can you believe that? It takes nearly 32,000 years, at 31.5 million seconds per year, to equal 1 trillion seconds. Or another way to look at this is, you would have to spend $31.5 million a year for 31,710 years just to spend $1 trillion.

The word "trillion" has been thrown around so much in the last few years that we have become numb to its vastness.

So, back to our debt – America's "real" debt currently stands at $76.1 trillion. This means that *your* personal share of this obligation is just over $250,000. That is the amount that every American would need to pay just to meet our *current* obligations. (Though by the time you read this book it will be much, much larger.)

Do you have an extra quarter million just sitting around under your mattress? A quarter million that you are eager to give the U.S. government? Does your 3-year-old son? Does your grandmother? Your great-uncle?

Every man, woman, and child in America would have to cough up $250,000, as of the writing of this book, to expunge this staggering mountain of obligation. And this number is growing at an unprecedented rate.

To make matters worse (not that we need to make them worse), if we calculate this debt based solely on the taxpaying citizens of the United States, the amount that each taxpayer would owe blossoms to *over $1 million – each!*[3]

Does that anger you in the same way it does me? It should. How is it possible that these cold, hard, facts would remain a secret to the American public? It should be headline news – every day. And while I'm not a conspiracy theorist, let's admit it, we've been lied to.

There is one person in public service that has been desperately trying to get this message out to the American people, but no one seems to be listening. As a matter of fact, it seems that most Americans have shoved their index fingers so far into their ears that their knuckles are touching somewhere in the middle of their heads.

The person I am referring to is David Walker, former comptroller general of the United States. For 15 years, and four presidential administrations, Mr. Walker served our country in different public capacities ranging from assistant secretary of labor for pension and welfare benefits to his final position as comptroller general of the United States.[4] Essentially, he was the nation's CPA.

What shocks me most about his message, other than its dire ramifications, is that no one is listening. Wouldn't you think that an appraisal from the man who had to sign off on America's budget would warrant our attention? Yet most Americans seem to choose ignorance.

Here are four quotes from Mr. Walker[5]:

> *"If [our country] were a company, we would be out of business."*

"Current federal financial reporting and budgeting provides policy-makers and the public with an incomplete and even a misleading picture."

"As the federal official who signs the audit report on the government's financial statements, it is apparent that our government's financial condition is far worse than advertised."

"We have been diagnosed with fiscal cancer."

These quotes are *not* taken out of context. The message is clear. We are in trouble, and if America doesn't make some quick changes, it will find itself on its financial knees, because what is yet to come is only going to exacerbate the already horrific problem.

Here's just one of the many reasons why:

In 1945 – five years after the first monthly payment was issued to a Social Security recipient – there were 42 workers per retiree. In 1950, the ratio was 16-to-1. In 1960, there were five workers per retiree. Today, the ratio is 3.3-to-1, and within 30 years, it is projected there will be just slightly more than two workers per retiree. Some economists have labeled Social Security a pyramid scheme.[6]

I find that last sentence a bit amusing, because it echoes a sentiment that an individual once shouted from the back of the room at one of my workshops. It was early in the workshop, and I was speaking about the pending problems surrounding Social Security. I was pointing out that there is absolutely *no* pot of money sitting *anywhere* within the Social Security program that has *your* name on it. None indeed. Social Security is a pay-as-you-go system. Every penny that is taken in each year is spent *that* year, including *your* Social Security tax. You are *not* putting money away for *you*. You are paying for the individuals currently receiving Social Security benefits.

As I was detailing this with the group, a man in the far back of the room yelled out, "It's just a Ponzi scheme!" Everyone laughed. Including me. His timing was perfect. You see, I was speaking at a hotel in downtown New York City to a group of local financial professionals, and Bernie Madoff had just been convicted of running the largest Ponzi scheme of all time. It was fresh on everyone's mind.

But you know what? I think the person who shouted that comment was right. Social Security *does* operate like a classic Ponzi scheme – a scheme that just may make Bernie's swindle look like a game of Monopoly®. (To be clear, I am not saying that Social Security *is* a Ponzi scheme. I'm simply saying that the parallels are very interesting.)

Let me give you the definition of a Ponzi scheme. Simply put, it is a scam that uses the money received from current depositors to pay back what is owed to the early depositors. This was the hoax Charles Ponzi perpetrated on a great number of people back in the 1920s. He had to keep generating new investment money from new individuals because little, if any, of the money he received from investors was actually ever invested. He simply used it to fund a lavish lifestyle.

This is not dissimilar to the way that Social Security works. As I just mentioned, all Social Security revenue that comes in during the current fiscal year is spent. However, it may be spent in ways that you were not aware. While it does cover benefits for existing retirees, it is also used to fund other parts of the government's over-committed general budget.

Yes, you heard me correctly. The government spends the money that you pay into the Social Security system on things *other than* Social Security.

The government borrows money from the Social Security Trust Fund so it can attempt to meet all of its other current obligations, and then it turns around and writes a big, fat IOU for what its just borrowed. Why does it do this? It must, in order to keep the doors of government open.

When you hear the term "Trust Fund," don't you think of a huge pot of money sitting somewhere, just waiting to be used? I do. However, that is not the case. It is a deceptive choice of words. The only reason there *is* a so-called Trust Fund is simply for accounting purposes, so the government knows how much it has borrowed from the Social Security program.

Do you see the similarity to a massive Ponzi scheme? Social Security takes *all* the current tax revenue from today's taxpayers to cover the benefits due to the earlier depositors, those who are now receiving Social Security benefits. The problem is, as you read above, pretty soon there are going to be only two workers for every one recipient of Social Security benefits. As my daughter would say, "Yeah, have fun with that."

Why does all this matter? I'll give you the answer in two words – future taxes. If our debt is almost *six times worse* than we thought, and the government's only source of revenue to combat this debt is taxation, then what do you think is going to happen to future tax rates? And if you don't think it is likely that tax rates will go up in the future, simply go back and review the tax rates in America over the last century. (See Appendix A for a year-by-year listing of the top marginal tax bracket all the way back to 1913.)

Did you know that back in the 1940s, the top marginal tax bracket was over 90 percent? No, that is not a typo. Over 90 percent! Think about what that means. It means that individuals paying taxes at that rate kept less than 10 cents out of every dollar they earned. Ninety cents or more of every dollar above that tax level went to Uncle Sam!

How would you like to keep only 10 cents of every hard-earned dollar? It is possible, you know. Unlikely, but possible. We *have* been there before; it's just that most people either don't remember or weren't alive to know.

So, does the significance of this debt issue, and its ramifications, make a little more sense now? I hope so.

But let me tell you, the best part is yet to come, because there *is* a solution for *your* retirement. A way you can potentially make future tax rates immaterial to your retirement savings. A way that you can get your money out of the tax-wash today and be able to access it tax-free in the future, regardless of at what age you want to retire*.

I know you may be thinking, "C'mon, that sounds too good to be true," but it's not. This strategy has been around for decades and is just as real and powerful today as ever. As a matter of fact, with the introduction of a new product in the marketplace, I believe the opportunity is *better* than ever. And this book, *The Retirement Miracle*, is going to give you the details about how this specific product works. I want you to see all the facts and then make the best informed decision that fits *you*, whether it utilizes this strategy or not.

This is *not* a one-size-fits-all approach; it is *not* for everybody. But for those that see its potential, and can afford to take advantage of its great benefits, I have found nothing better.

* Based on current tax law as of this writing.

Chapter 2

Storm Clouds on the Horizon

In May of 2007 I hosted my first training workshop for financial professionals. At that event I gave each attendee a notebook of materials for the day that was divided into five areas of financial concern, or "storm clouds," as I called them.

The first two categories dealt with debt, both personal and national. What I saw concerned me. The last category centered on the foreclosure activity I saw accelerating around the country, especially in the state of Ohio at the time.

I made a statement to that small group (which I still have on video) in which I warned that very soon something was going to set an inferno ablaze within the economy. While I didn't know with certainty what it would be, I speculated that very possibly it would be ignited by foreclosures.

That was 18 months *before* the actual housing meltdown; I had no idea how right that prediction was going to prove. (Trust me, I wish I'd been wrong.) And that ensuing devastation, set off by foreclosures, just about brought down the entire world economy. Literally.

How did I make that statement a year and a half before it happened? Simple. Storm clouds. Very dark storm clouds. I'm neither a prophet nor a meteorologist, but one thing I've learned from living in the Northwest all my life is this: If you see a dark cloud coming your way, it's likely going to rain.

Yeah, I know, that's profound. But you'd be surprised how many people miss the obvious. I know some individuals who wouldn't see an elephant if it sat on their head.

The storm clouds I saw brewing back in 2007 were pretty daunting. When my wife and I bought our first house, the only institutions that seemed to offer financing for my loan were traditional banks. You know, the kind where you deposit money, have a checking account, and know the local teller. Getting a loan took an act of Congress and almost as much paper.

But in the new housing marketplace of the 21st century, everything had changed. People were getting rich. House values were soaring. There was no need for archaic processes like underwriting or income verification. This was a new era. And no one wanted in on the profits more than Wall Street's investment banks. They couldn't stand to sit on the sidelines and watch everyone else get rich. Making money was their game, and they not only wanted to play, they wanted to write the rules. And so they did.

And what did these "Titans of Finance" create? The "100-percent financing, No-Doc, Stated Income, Negative Amortizing" loan. I laugh as I write this. Literally, a person could wrap all those features into one loan. It was beyond comical. It was insane. And what do these terms actually mean?

- **100-percent financing:** The buyers didn't need to contribute a single dime to actually purchase the house.

They could finance it all, transferring all of the risk to the financial institutions.

- **No-Doc:** The banks didn't verify such silly things as job status or credit history. Nope. If you could sign your name, you could buy a home.
- **Stated Income:** The clients told the banks how much they made. In other words, they lied.
- **Negative Amortizing:** The clients payments wouldn't be large enough to even cover the monthly interest, so the principle balance on the loan would increase each month, putting them further and further into debt

It was the new age of easy money. Anyone could get a loan for virtually any house he wanted. I remember meeting with a mortgage broker in our town to look at buying a house that I knew was likely beyond our budget. I was really just dipping my toe into the water at this point. It was a Saturday afternoon, and he agreed to meet me at his office. I pulled out the flier for the house I was interested in and shared that I didn't think my income would allow me to qualify.

His answer. "Oh yeah, you'll qualify. We can do a stated income application. You can just put down whatever you want."

Something smelled fishy. I said, "*Seriously*, I can just tell them whatever I want?"

"Yep."

"How are they able to do that?" I asked. "Don't they verify it?"

"Well, it's supposed to be verifiable, but trust me, they never do. Even if they did, once you bought the house and they had already approved it, there's really nothing they could do. It wouldn't even be a slap on the hand. Everyone's doing it right now. It's my most popular loan."

After looking at this loan program and thinking about the house, we decided to pass. But, his last two statements set off caution alarms in my head.

"Everyone's doing it right now."

"It's my most popular loan."

Do you remember the title of chapter seven in my first book, "Land Mine #5 – Following the masses"? Usually when everyone is doing it, that spells trouble.

You see, economic principles were being grossly breached, and laws of finance are no different than Newton's Law of Gravity; neither can be violated for long without eventually crashing back to earth. Not only had the mortgage industry thrown all common sense to the wind, but it was allowing people to let greed drive their decisions. And that's a deadly combo.

Why is any of this important to the issue at hand? Because the very same storm clouds that were on the horizon of the credit crisis now loom over our nation's entire economy. If we don't get a handle on the problem, the rain will come, and the resulting flood would give even Noah a run for his money.

Let me tell you, the crisis the world experienced with the credit freeze of 2008 will seem a mere preschool event compared to the disaster that would ensue from a seizure of America's credit machine. It would be a cataclysm of apocalyptic proportions.

Now, do I think we are going to let this happen? No.

At least I certainly hope not. But, if we are going to avert this catastrophe, there are only two things we can do as a country.

No. 1: Spend less.

No. 2: Tax more.

Which one do *you* think is likely?

As I look at what's on the political agenda right now, I don't see spending slowing any time soon. Take a look at an article from early 2010:

> *The spending blueprint forecasts this year's budget shortfall will hit a record $1.6 trillion, following a $1.4 trillion deficit in 2009. The 2011 deficit, for the fiscal year that starts Oct. 1, is predicted to be $1.3 trillion, with deficits remaining above $700 billion for the rest of the decade, according to the projections.*[7]

To avert disaster, it is my opinion, as well as that of most individuals I have ever asked, that taxes *must* go up. Let's just hope that if they do, at least *some* of the money actually makes it to its intended destination, and that we begin to chip away at this tsunami of debt.

Chapter 3

Can Anyone Escape?

Right about now, you may be saying to yourself, "Wow, I'm sure glad I picked up this book! Nothing quite like an encouraging shot in the arm."

But don't lose heart. The reason I'm sharing this information is very important. If you don't completely understand the magnitude of the problem, you won't fully appreciate the incredible power of the solution. So, hang with me for a couple more chapters, because there is another topic we need to examine, and that is the traditional wisdom of the "buy-and-hold" strategy.

If you've ever read any books or articles on investing, a common theme in many of them is to simply apply a "buy-and-hold" strategy to your long-term investments. In other words, what these pundits are saying is, "*Don't panic when the market goes down. Don't jettison your investments. Just hang in there and ride it out.*" Yeah, just like Gilligan's little three-hour cruise.

There is one aspect of their message I do agree with. It is this – don't try and time the markets. Trust me. The markets will always make you look foolish, and you will eventually get on the wrong side of the equation, costing you lots of money. However, beyond that one nugget of truth, I think this investment strategy may be nearing extinction. Why? Because the "buy-and-hold" strategy is predicated on one very important principle: *The market must return to new highs.*

But, what if that is not the case? What if a bear market (one that goes down) were to last for 20 years? Does a traditional "buy-and-hold" strategy work in that environment?

Well, let's take a look. Let's consider the world's third-largest economy behind the United States and China – Japan. Wikipedia, one of my favorite online information sources, says regarding Japan's leading stock index, the Nikkei 225:

> *The Nikkei average hit its all-time high on December 29, 1989, during the peak of the Japanese asset price bubble, when it reached an intra-day high of 38,957.44 before closing at 38,915.87. Its high for the 21st century stands just above 18,300 points. In January 2010, it was 72.9 percent below its peak.*[8]

Now, as I write this chapter, almost 21 years after it touched its all-time high, the Nikkei 225 index stands at just 9,346.13 – still 76 percent below its closing high over two decades ago. See chart across.

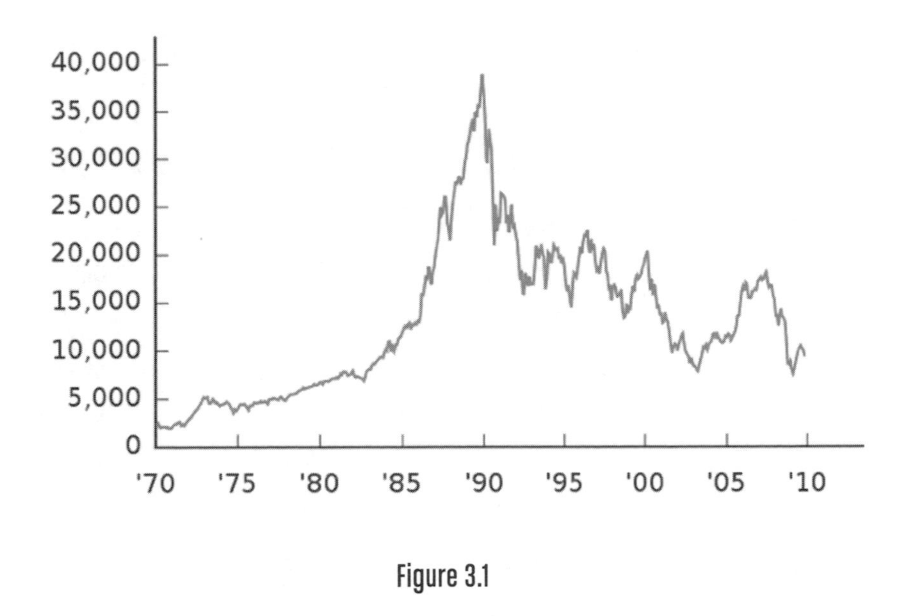

Figure 3.1

Did you catch that? Japan's leading stock index (like our S&P 500 index) is ***still down*** 76 percent, more than 20 years after it hit its peak.

Part of the reason I'm using Japan as an example is because its economy went through in 1990 a situation similar to what America is going through today. We could learn much from its experience.

So, how did the "buy and hold" strategy work for those Japanese investors who placed their money in the market back in December 1989? That's right, they have still lost 76 percent of their money after two decades of holding tough.

Let me show you, graphically, what $1,000 would have been worth each year, through year-end 2009, if it had simply been left in that market, tracking the Nikkei 225 index. See figure 3.2 on next page.

The value of $1,000 in the Nikkei 225 from 12/31/1989 to 12/31/2009

YEAR	END OF YEAR CLOSE	ANNUAL RETURN	VALUE OF $1,000
1989	38,915.90	NA	$1,000.00
1990	23,848.70	-38.72	$612.83
1991	22,983.80	-3.63	$590.60
1992	16,925.00	-26.36	$434.91
1993	17,417.20	2.91	$447.56
1994	19,723.10	13.24	$506.81
1995	19,868.20	0.74	$510.54
1996	19,361.30	-2.55	$497.52
1997	15,258.70	-21.19	$392.09
1998	13,842.17	-9.28	$355.69
1999	18,934.34	36.79	$486.55
2000	13,785.69	-27.19	$354.24
2001	10,542.60	-23.53	$270.91
2002	8,578.95	-18.63	$220.45
2003	10,676.60	24.45	$274.35
2004	11,488.76	7.61	$295.22
2005	16,111.43	40.24	$414.01
2006	17,225.83	6.92	$442.64
2007	15,307.78	-11.13	$393.36
2008	8,859.56	-42.12	$227.66
2009	10,546.44	19.04	$271.01

Figure 3.2

That $1,000 of value in December of 1989 would be worth a measly $271 at year-end December 2009. After two full decades! And that doesn't take into account the further, and significant, erosion from inflation.

As a side note, the Nikkei 225 is down an additional 11.38 percent in 2010, as this book is getting ready to go to press. So that $271 has diminished even further, to $240.16. It just keeps going and going, but in the *wrong* direction.

However, even though the *total return* through the end of 2009 is a negative 73.8 percent, you will see that many of the *individual* years (nine to be exact) *did* produce a positive return; some of them very robust. Take 2005 for example. The return for the index that year was a whopping 40.24 percent. The problem is that in 2007 and 2008 the market took it all back – and then some.

You see, the traditional "buy-and-hold" strategy has no way of capturing those individual years of positive gain without factoring in all the negative years as well. Yet, the self-proclaimed investment gurus would tell you to just hold on. Ride it out. Take on a little more water. Yes, your ship may be sinking, but traditional wisdom says that all captains must go down with their ship.

By the way, who came up with that brilliant idea? I can guarantee it was *not* the captain; rather, it was likely a passenger who wanted a spot in the last remaining lifeboat.

Now, let's have some fun. Let's play around a bit. Let's adjust the returns we just looked at in the chart above by two factors. First, let's remove all negative years and make them simply zero – neither loss nor gain. Second, let's limit the gain in any single year to a maximum of 14 percent.

Now, before you inquire as to *why* we are doing this, let's first look at those numbers. The difference is staggering.

The value of $1,000 in the Nikkei 225 from 12/31/1989 to 12/31/2009(removing all negative years and capping returns at 14 percent)

YEAR	END OF YEAR CLOSE	ANNUAL RETURN	VALUE OF $1,000
1989	38915.90	BeginningYear	$1,000.00
1990	23848.70	0.00	$1,000.00
1991	22983.80	0.00	$1,000.00
1992	16925.00	0.00	$1,000.00
1993	17417.20	2.91	$1,029.10
1994	19723.10	13.24	$1,165.35
1995	19868.20	0.74	$1,173.98
1996	19361.30	0.00	$1,173.98
1997	15258.70	0.00	$1,173.98
1998	13842.17	0.00	$1,173.98
1999	18934.34	14.00	$1,338.33
2000	13785.69	0.00	$1,338.33
2001	10542.60	0.00	$1,338.33
2002	8578.95	0.00	$1,338.33
2003	10676.60	14.00	$1,525.70
2004	11488.76	7.61	$1,641.81
2005	16111.43	14.00	$1,871.66
2006	17225.83	6.92	$2,001.18
2007	15307.78	0.00	$2,001.18
2008	8859.56	0.00	$2,001.18
2009	10546.44	14.00	$2,281.34

Figure 3.3

Can you believe the difference? Only nine years had positive gains, and not one of them achieved greater than a 14 percent return; yet the amount of money that an individual would have in *this* scenario is 742 percent more than simply letting it ride with the traditional "buy-and-hold" strategy: $2,281 versus $271. Which amount would you prefer after 20 years?

How was this immense anomaly possible? Simple. The second account ***never took losses.***

One thing I strongly believe. *Protect your investment capital at all costs!* That should be your No. 1 principle for wealth accumulation. As a matter of fact, if that was your *only* principle, you'd be better off than most. Trust me, I've learned this the hard way. Don't make my mistakes.

Can you believe the difference that simply eliminating the negative years makes? It's astounding. But what if there *was* a way you could do exactly that? A way to:

1. Capture each year of positive gain, up to a certain cap, *AND*
2. Eliminate each negative year, making your worst possible return 0 percent

Sounds impossible, doesn't it? Well, the good news, no the *great* news, is that it's not only possible, it's actually quite easy. There ***is*** a product that will allow you to do exactly that.

Chapter 4

A Rocky Beginning

That product is called Indexed Universal Life Insurance.

Indexed Universal Life is an amazing product with incredible features and benefits. However, before you can fully appreciate how this life insurance policy differs from the two versions of Universal Life that preceded it, I must take you on a brief journey through Universal Life's tumultuous, three-decade history.

Can you think of anything more fun than a history lesson on life insurance? That's right up there with counting the blades of grass in your back lawn. Sorry, but it's necessary – and I'll try to make it fun.

Traditional Universal Life

The very first Universal Life policy was introduced back in the early 1980s and, quite frankly, there couldn't have been a worse time to bring the product to market. Why? Interest rates.

If you looked at the history of interest rates all the way back to 1929, you would see that the prime rate has spent most of its time in the single-digit range, even as low as 1.5 percent in the 1930s, during the Great Depression.

However, there was a period of roughly six years – five years and seven months to be exact – when the prime rate was in double-digit territory the entire time. Those months ranged from October 1978 to May 1984. It peaked in July of 1981 at a high of 20.5 percent.

And you know what was introduced right in the middle of these historically high interest rates? You guessed it. The very first Universal Life policy.

Now, why was this a problem?

It was a problem for a number of reasons. First and foremost, a Traditional Universal Life policy's growth is based on interest rates, and an illustration on that policy is simply a *projection*, not a guarantee. And guess what interest rates were used to project how the policy would perform in future years? If you said the current rate at the time the policy was purchased, you'd be correct. In other words, agents were showing clients illustrations that projected their policy would return 13 percent or 14 percent – forever. How realistic was that?

So, when the first UL was introduced with an interest rate in the teens, the projections were off the charts. It looked like a financial wonder drug. Everyone was going to get rich.

But then in June of 1984, interest rates began to fall ... and fall ... and fall ... and fall some more. This meant the actual return those early policies experienced would come far short of those lofty projections, because high interest rates were taking the path of the dinosaur. Since its peak in

July of 1981, the prime rate has fallen nearly every year, all the way down to where it stands today – 3.25 percent.

And guess what happened to that supposed panacea, Traditional Universal Life? That's right. The interest rate it achieved fell far short of those supercharged projections when interest rates were in the teens.

And if that wasn't bad enough – and here's where the real problem occurred – agents ran for cover. I think the carnage could have been mollified a bit if agents would have just stayed consistent in reviewing their customers' policies, but most didn't. Many had egg on their face, because they had misrepresented the policy to begin with, not intentionally I'm sure, but misrepresented none-the-less. Clients assumed the high interest rates shown on their original illustrations were how this policy would actually perform, instead of just the *hypothetical* projection that they were. And once these policies started imploding, agents ran for the hills.

During a break at one of my workshops, an agent approached me and asked, "Hey Patrick, have you heard of Vanishing Premium Life?" I paused, waiting for the punch-line I knew was coming. "That's when an agent sells a policy and then vanishes." We chuckled at the joke, but we both knew that buried within that humor was a real nugget of disastrous truth because, unfortunately, that is exactly what many agents did. And what was the result? A blood bath for both the consumer, whose policies began to lapse, and the life insurance companies, who faced a bevy of class-action lawsuits.

And lost in the middle of it all was this fantastic (though beaten and haggard) product called Traditional Universal Life.

Let me interject this important thought, something all

potential life insurance purchasers should understand, something I've said to my clients for years. It's this: There's only one thing you can be guaranteed about *any* illustration – only one thing. That it's going to be *wrong*. Why? Because an illustration simply shows one possible scenario of what *could* happen given one specific set of parameters. It is how this policy would look if it achieved the exact same rate of return every year, for the next 50-plus years, and of course we know that's not going to happen. It may perform better. It may perform worse. You won't know for sure until you get back together with your advisor and review your policy each year. However, the one thing you can be assured of is that this illustration will *not* be correct. It's a hypothetical projection, not a guarantee.

Let me give you an analogy. Let's say a friend of yours asks you to come with him to pick up his dream car, a Porsche 911 Turbo. It's a beauty. Fast. Sleek. Built to drive. You jump at the chance, because you've always wanted to ride in one.

You show up at the dealership, and there, parked right in front of the shop, is his car. Bright red and glimmering in the noon-day sun. All the paperwork is complete, so all you need to do is get in and drive off. As you ease yourself down into the passenger seat, you take in the delightful aroma of the high-end leather. Your friend fires up the engine and the car comes to life like a fighter jet. He puts the car in gear, looks both ways, and rockets into the street. It's a thing of beauty. The ride of your life. Very few cars are built better than the one you're in. (Sorry, I'm a car nut getting lost in my own reverie.)

He launches down the onramp and onto the freeway, and before you know it, you're doing 100 mph. You shouldn't be, but you are. But since it would be his ticket and not yours, you sit back in silence, a smile stretching from ear to ear, and let him drive.

You look over again and you're now approaching 150 mph. You watch your friend reach down to shift from fifth to sixth gear, but instead he does the unthinkable. Something tragic happens. Instead of shifting into sixth gear, he messes up. He has a total lapse of mental capacity. And what enfolds before you happens as if in slow motion. Instead of shifting into the next gear, he slams the car into reverse ... at triple-digit speeds.

Can you picture the scene? Complete disaster. A horrible noise, a ruined engine, and pieces of the German car scattered all over the roadway.

But then, an even more amazing thing happens. As the car is sputtering its last mechanical gasp, your friend turns to you and says, "Can you believe that!? A brand new Porsche and it breaks down on the first day! I'm taking it back to the dealer! I want my money back!"

As you sit there in stunned amazement, you think to yourself, *Now there's a dude whose elevator doesn't reach the top floor.*

Ridiculous, isn't it? You would *never* blame the car for breaking down due to operator error. But that's exactly what happened in the case of Universal Life. It is a *wonderful* product, and it performed exactly as it was designed. The problem wasn't the product, rather, it was operator error. It was improperly sold by many agents and then abandoned, left to die, never having a chance to get back on track. The industry was chasing the high-interest-rate environment of the 1980s, and caught it right at the tail end. A raw deal for all parties involved.

As a sidebar, I want to make a note of two things. One, I am a firm believer in regular and consistent reviews for *all* financial products. That is the key to staying on track. And two, with interest rates right now at historic *lows*, I think the future of Traditional Universal Life could be the opposite of its past. If interest rates go back up down the road, and likely they will, then the performance of these current policies could end up being better than what they currently project. Just a thought to keep in mind. But as always, only the future can prove that true.

So, what happened next? To the rescue comes – Variable Universal Life.

Variable Universal Life

Since the interest-rate approach imploded, and the stock market was soaring to new highs, the life insurance industry wanted to create a way for its clients to take advantage of that growth within their life insurance contracts.

Just so life insurance companies don't get vilified in this short history, it is my personal belief that they likely didn't want to bring this product to market at all, but did so purely out of customer demand. Remember, there was a period, not long ago, in which complete neophytes were making millions in the stock market. That's the *only* place many people would even *think* of putting their money. So, to give its future customers that opportunity, the insurance industry introduced the Variable Universal Life policy (known as VUL).

The difference between this policy and its older brother, the Traditional UL, is that the returns within this policy are based on stock market performance, both the positive *and* the negative. (A small but important feature that many agents forgot to mention.)

And just as people in the early '80s ignored the fact that interest rates can go down, people of the '90s brushed off the fact that stock market returns don't always go up. Once again, the industry was arriving late to the dance.

The first VUL was introduced right in the middle of one of the stock market's longest bull runs. Unlike the interest rate version, the VUL also came burdened with higher fees and expenses, due to the administrative costs incurred by the companies providing the policy. However, with strong stock market returns, those expenses were hardly noticed.

The problem, of course, is that markets don't always go up. (Duh!) And just like the first round of the Traditional UL, market conditions changed, and changed rapidly.

On March 10, 2000, the NASDAQ Composite hit its all-time high of 5,132.52. The following Monday, on March 13, 2000, the NASDAQ opened 4 percent lower than it had closed on the previous Friday. Look what happened:

> *The massive initial batch of sell orders processed on Monday, March 13 triggered a chain reaction of selling that fed on itself as investors, funds, and institutions liquidated positions. In just six days the NASDAQ had lost nearly nine percent, falling from roughly 5,050 on March 10 to 4,580 on March 15...*
>
> *By 2001 the bubble was deflating at full speed. A majority of the dot-coms ceased trading after burning through their venture capital, many having never made a net profit. Investors often jokingly referred to these failed dot-coms as "dot-bombs".*[9]

As of December 13, 2010, nearly 11 years after touching its all-time high, the NASDAQ composite closed at 2,624.91. It is *still* 49 percent *below* its peak!

You see, stock markets go up, and stock markets go down. And often they go in one direction for a very long time. Just ask Japan.

And while the VUL can be a very good tool in a rising market environment, it can be a disaster in a negative-market environment. Why? Because, as the policy's cash value is decreasing due to market conditions, the costs associated with the life insurance policy (i.e., policy fees as well as death benefit costs) are still being charged and paid for out of declining asset values within the policy, rapidly ensuring it's demise.

Again, the VUL can serve a good purpose; however, an individual must know the inherent risks going into it, *and*, as I mentioned earlier in this chapter, consumers *must* review their policies on a regular basis.

With this track record, is it any wonder that Universal Life has gotten such a bad rap?

But, as they say, the third time's a charm!

Chapter 5

The Solution

So, what type of policy could possibly come next? We've seen an interest-rate product. We've seen an equity-based product. What else can there be? Like I said, the third time's a charm.

Since companies were no longer chasing the next hot crediting method, I believe they were able to step back and really study what worked and what didn't work with the previous two policy types. And what they came up with was a blend of the two. And not just any blend. The ideal blend. The result? The Indexed Universal Life policy. And let me tell you, this ain't your daddy's life insurance!

This policy was introduced to the market around 1995. So why haven't you heard about it? Because many agents had such a poor experience with the first two versions, I think many lumped all Universal Life Policies into one big group, and shunned them like a mangy dog. And if the agents who are able to sell the policy aren't going to tell you about it, then who will?

Honestly, if you were to ask me to name one single negative about this policy, I couldn't. Not one. (And I can point out many shortcomings of its two older brothers.) It's a wonderful genetic mix of its parents' best attributes. In my opinion, this time the insurance industry got it right. No, better than right – impeccable!

And quite frankly, in my opinion, the No. 1 benefit this policy provides isn't even mentioned in any company's sales literature – *peace of mind!*

In the rest of this chapter I will give you a brief overview of this policy and many of its remarkable benefits, without leading you into a miry swamp of complicated and distracting numbers.

Here's a quick thumbnail explanation of 15 characteristics that are common to virtually all Indexed Universal Life policies:

1. **Death Benefit** – The crown jewel of all life insurance policies is, and always will be, the death benefit that it provides to the policy owner's beneficiary. Really, when you think about it, this feature in itself is a bit of a miracle. For pennies on the dollar, individuals are able to buy protection for their family that will ensure their family can continue in the lifestyle they are accustomed to, even if the income earner was to die prematurely. That is one important benefit ... just ask any widow who was left without it.

2. **Cash accumulation** – Just like most cash-value life insurance policies, the Indexed Universal Life policy (IUL) provides the potential for cash accumulation within the policy. This cash can be accessed and used at the policy owner's discretion. The individual can always make a tax-free withdrawal, up to the total amount of premiums they

have paid into the policy, since this withdrawal simply represents a return of the after-tax money that he originally contributed to the policy.

3. **Protection against market loss** – Without a doubt, this is one of the most incredible features of an IUL. This policy contractually *guarantees* that your cash value will *never* ... yes, I did say *never* ... have a negative return due to market losses – ever. Wow! Do you remember how significant that was when we looked at the Japanese Nikkei 225 example in chapter three? It's huge. That one factor made a 742-percent difference. I'll explain in more detail in chapter 12, how the companies are able to provide this type of protection. But for now, just know that it is true, and it is powerful. Who *wouldn't* give up a little of their upside gain to insure that they never had a losing year?

4. **The Annual Reset Provision** – If the IUL had a "Secret Sauce," this would be it in my opinion. The Annual Reset Provision allows an individual to capture, and more importantly, *lock in* each year of positive return in the market. So, if a policyholder's cash value increased by 10 percent in a given year, at the time of the policy's anniversary, this 10 percent gain would now become the new protected amount within the policy, even if the markets were to go down in the future. Another way to think of it is this: *The annual growth to a policy's cash value is the policyholder's to keep forever. It can never be taken away due to negative market performance.* So, not only is a policyholder's initial cash value contribution protected from loss, but the annual growth is as well.

5. **Upside growth potential** – Protecting your capital against loss is vitally important, but so is knowing your account can also experience the potential for decent growth. We all want to know there is room for growth. And there is. While each company sets its own ceiling on growth (called a cap), the industry as a whole is hovering somewhere in the low to mid teens as of this writing. So how does this all play out? If the stock market index that your policy is tracking (often the S&P 500) goes up 5 percent in a given year, then the money in your cash value will also grow approximately 5 percent. If the index increases by 11 percent, then, likewise, your return will be around 11 percent. However, if the market has a banner (and unusual) year and goes up by 24 percent, you will be limited to the maximum cap rate of whatever that particular company offers. In the case of a company that offers a cap of 14 percent, your annual gain that year will be limited to the maximum amount of 14 percent.

6. **Tax-Deferred Growth** – It's very important for individuals to understand that life insurance cash values grow tax-deferred, *not* tax-free. In other words, if someone were to simply *withdraw* all of his or her funds, or *cancel* the policy, especially in the later years, then all of the gain (the amount above the total premium payments) *would be* subject to tax – income tax, not capital gains tax. HOWEVER, life insurance companies have designed a way for individuals to gain *access* to an equivalent of the cash value amount, completely tax-free. Let's look at No. 7 below.

7. **Tax-free access to cash accumulation** – Let me ask you a question. When you go to buy a car, is the loan you take out for that car taxed? No. The car may be taxed, but the loan is not. It's also true with a house, a boat, or any other loan. Loans aren't taxed. This principle holds true for life insurance as well. Life insurance companies have designed a brilliant way for you to be able to *access* an equivalent of your cash value ... tax-free. It's simply called the Policy Loan Provision. This feature, and the way in which it works, is so vital that I'm going to spend all of chapter nine explaining it in detail.

8. **No minimum age or income requirement** – Unlike tax-qualified plans, such as a SEP IRA, life insurance has no minimum age that an individual must attain to put this strategy into place. Nor does an individual need to have earned income in order to contribute. For example, I have purchased a policy for my four children within the first month of each of their lives. This can supercharge results because it enables you to add 20 or more years of tax-deferred growth to the account. The results are stunning.

9. **No mandatory distribution** – One of the many problems of saving money in a tax-qualified plan, like an IRA or 401(k), is that, not long after you turn 70, you are forced to begin liquidating the account whether you need the money or not. It's not hard to guess why that rule exists. The government doesn't get paid (i.e., tax) until you start *withdrawing* money. So, it forces you to begin withdrawals in order to get their hands on the portion of your retirement account that it essentially

owns – the tax. Make sense? The IUL, however, does not come burdened with this or with most of the other bureaucratic red tape of traditional tax-qualified plans. *You* get to decide how and when to use your money – not Uncle Sam.

10. **Access at any age** – It seems to me that one of the main reasons people currently choose to retire at age 60 and older is because, utilizing tax-qualified plans, they must be at least that old to get at their money without paying steep tax penalties. Not so with the IUL. Your money is accessible at any age, leaving 100 percent of the decision up to you.

11. **Protection from lawsuits (in many states)** – It is common, in many states, that the cash value accumulated inside of a life insurance policy is protected from creditors, whether that is due to bankruptcy, lawsuit, or another type of judgment. This is one benefit you don't hear spoken about very often, likely because many practitioners don't know this, and also because this law can vary from state to state. However, for individuals in high-income professions, especially physicians, due to the threat of a malpractice suit, this can be one of the most significant features of the policy. Make sure to check the laws within your own state.

12. **Continued Investment if Disabled** – Another optional feature I want to let you know about is called Waiver of Premium for Disability. While the name describes the benefit well, new versions of this benefit extend beyond the

obvious. I think it would be safe to say that virtually all companies offer this benefit in its basic form, which simply provides a continuation of your premium payments in order to keep the life insurance in force if you were to become permanently disabled. (Each company has its own definition of "disability," so make sure and check your specific policy.) However, many companies have extended that benefit even further and allow you to select an option (with additional cost, of course) that will not only pay to keep the life insurance death benefit in force, but will also continue to fund the policy at your current contribution amount, up to a certain level. How many financial vehicles do you know that have an auto-continuation of your monthly contribution if you happen to become disabled? Yeah, I thought so.

13. **Does not create taxation of Social Security Benefits** – What many people don't know is that a great percentage of their Social Security benefits can now be subject to income taxation when it is received, based upon where their other retirement income is derived. All money that comes from a tax-qualified plan [401(k), SEP, SIMPLE, IRA, etc.] during retirement will be included as income that can negatively effect the income taxation of an individual's Social Security benefit. Here's the good news. Income coming out of a cash-value life insurance policy, whether it be via withdrawal or loan, does *not* subject an individual's Social Security to income taxation. That can be very significant.

14. **Avoids Probate** – This says it all. Because a life insurance policy is a contract that has a named beneficiary, the death benefit is paid directly to that beneficiary within days of the death of the insured. It does not get tied up in probate or other legal battles. It is quick, simple, easy, and immediate. Contrast that with the lengthy and difficult delay that probate can impose on the rest of a deceased's estate.

15. **Accurate Return Figures** – The returns that are reported by most financial products are simply smoke and mirrors. A shadow of their reality. This feature is so compelling, however, that I want to devote the entire next chapter to its significance. I hope you're sitting down.

Chapter 6

The Big Lie

Sometimes a lie is told so well that even its perpetrators believe it. Such is the case with stock market averages.

Let me see, how can I convey this next thought nicely, gently, in a way that doesn't offend anyone? Sorry – I can't. Here's the bitter truth. *It's a lie! Fiction. The "average" returns reported by financial companies are not reality. They're just smoke and mirrors.*

Sorry; that was as nice as I could be. It's infuriating. The sad part is that I think most of the folks in the financial industry don't understand what I'm about to tell you. And if they do, shame on them.

Here's the scoop. Most stock market benchmarks (indexes as they are called, like the *Dow Jones Industrial*, the *S&P 500*, the *Russell 2000*), as well as most mutual funds, tout their *average* returns over given periods of time. One year. Three year. Five year. And lifetime. They post them on their fact sheets. They share them with the media. It's what most (dare I say all) financial professionals preach to their clients.

"Yes, Mr. and Mrs. Client, the S&P 500 has returned an average of 10.16 percent over the last 20 years,[10] even when you include the terrible results of 2008."

Hogwash! The statement may be *factually* true, but in reality it's misleading – worthless.

Why? Simple. There is a huge difference between the *average* return and the *actual* return. To illustrate, I'm going to ask you a question. A question that at first glance seems ridiculously simple. Silly even. But this question could be one of the most powerful concepts you could grasp in order to take control of your financial future. Here it is.

> *If a person invests $1,000 into an account and this account experiences a negative-50-percent return in year one and a positive-50-percent return in year two, how much money would be in the account at the end of the second year?*

Think about it for a second. The average return is zero, right?

Year 1 Year 2

$$\frac{(-50\%) + 50\%}{2} = \frac{0}{2} = 0\% \text{ Average}$$

[figure 6.1]

Well, if the average return is 0 percent (which it is), then wouldn't the ending value be equal to its beginning value of $1,000?

Nope. Not even close.

The ***average*** return may be 0 percent, but the ***actual*** return is negative 25 percent!

What!? How can that be?

Let me illustrate using the numbers. If a person invests $1,000 into an account, and in the first year it experiences a negative-50-percent return, then that $1,000 drops to $500, correct?

$1,000 less 50% = $500

($500)

[figure 6.2] (50 percent of $1,000 is $500.)

Now, if that account has a positive 50-percent gain in year two, it would increase back up to $750.

$500 plus 50% = $750

($250)

[figure 6.3] (50 percent of $500 is $250. $500 + $250 = $750.)

So, at the end of two years, even though the average return is 0 percent, the account actually experienced a 25-percent drop.

How can this be true? If the average return is zero, how can the ending value be significantly less? Why aren't these values the same? It's very simple:

> *The "actual" return and the "average" return will NEVER equal one another anytime you have to factor in a negative number.*

In other words, if you *ever* have to factor in a negative year's result (the year in which a market went down), then the *average* return (the number often boasted to the public) and the *actual* return (the amount that an account or fund actually experienced) will *never* be the same.

So, since markets *do* experience negative years, the averaging method just doesn't work. It's not an accurate picture of how a market or account has really performed; unless, of course, every year during that period has experienced a positive return.

What this means is that even though an investment could claim an *average* return of 0 percent in the example above, which would be a factual statement (allowing individuals to think they haven't lost any money), the client would have experienced an actual *loss* of 25 percent of his investment.

So, let's revisit that hypothetical statement made by the financial professional earlier in this chapter. "Yes, Mr. & Mrs. Client, the S&P 500 has returned an average of 10.16 percent over the last 20 years, even when you include the terrible results of 2008." That statement would make an individual think that his accounts have *experienced* an actual growth of 10.16 percent. Right? Of course. What else could he think?

However, in the scenario above, the *actual (real)* return this client experienced over the last 20 years, the actual growth to his account, is only 8.23 percent (5.36 percent if you include inflation.)[11]

If you want to easily see these differences for yourself, I want to direct you to a great website I found called MoneyChimp.com. At this website, *http://www.moneychimp.com/features/market_cagr.htm*, you will be able to enter any range of years and see the average versus the actual return. Powerful stuff.

So why is this important? Because by using the Indexed *strategy*, you *never* have to factor in any negative numbers, because *this strategy is contractually guaranteed to NEVER have a negative return. EVER. Not in any year. No matter how much a stock market goes down. The worst you can do in any given year is zero*, and with some products it can be even better than that.

As the saying in the industry goes, "Zero is your hero."

Therefore, while the "average return" is complete fiction in regard to the stock market, mutual funds, and the like, it *is* accurate for Indexed products since this product never, ever, ever has to factor in a negative year's return.

Now that's something to get excited about.

Chapter 7

But I Heard Life Insurance is a Bad Investment

I just had to include this chapter in my book. Why? Because its title is the single most common statement I've heard over the years regarding life insurance as a wealth-building tool: "But I heard life insurance is a bad investment." When people make that statement, I love to turn the question back to them.

I'll ask, "Really? Why do you think so?"

Almost always, without fail, they sit there quietly like a Michelangelo statue. They don't know. They can't come up with an answer. They have no facts to back up their declaration. Most of the time they have never even looked into it themselves.

The only reason they make such a statement is because they are simply mimicking the words of someone they have heard, likely on radio or television. They've never looked into the facts themselves. It's just the simple spewing of an unverified and uneducated statement.

Sorry, I know this sounds harsh, but come on, if someone's going to make a blanket statement like that, he better be able to rustle up at least one factual rebuttal. (Now, just for the record, I don't make them feel badly. As a matter of fact, I don't make them squirm. Not even a little. I'm nice and let them off easy.) But now you know how I *really* feel.

So, let's address a couple of important things.

First and foremost, *life insurance is **not** an investment*–at least not in the traditional sense. It is life insurance, meaning that the first and most important part of the policy will always be the death benefit provided to the insured's beneficiaries.

Life insurance companies get all puckered up whenever they hear the words "investment" and "life insurance" in the same sentence. And for good reason. They believe in full disclosure, and definitely want to make sure the client knows that part of the premium payment is going toward the purchase of a product (fees, expenses, and the cost of the insurance itself) and not just to future savings.

Life insurance and investments are different animals altogether. Different fish, if you will. However, both of these fish are swimming in the same ocean.

Let me explain. A primary reason that life insurance shouldn't be called an investment is because the policy owner is buying a product (a death benefit) that eats up part of his or her capital, unlike putting money in the bank. So, dollar for dollar, all other things being equal (growth rate, tax rate, etc.), money deposited into a true investment will generally outperform money put into a life insurance contract, because the death benefit in the life insurance contract eats up part of the premium paid.

However, and this is a *big* however, all things are *not* generally equal, and this is what gives life insurance, particularly Indexed Universal Life Insurance, some of its amazing advantages.

Let's break this down. While the primary reason to purchase life insurance will always be the death benefit that it provides, life insurance *also* provides many living advantages to the policy owner as well. Advantages that if utilized properly, can be a complete game changer.

The second reason I believe that people make the erroneous assertion that "life insurance is a bad investment" is because the media has misled them. As a general rule, I've found the information purported by the media to be one step above toxic, at least in regards to life insurance's full slate of benefits. But, the media isn't the only culprit.

I have had the privilege in the last few years to train thousands of the life insurance industry's top producers – men and women who have made this work their life's calling. As a matter of fact, I can think of a few I've met who have put in more than five decades – yes, over 50 years!

And yet, when I do a training, even for those who are lifetime professionals, a good majority of the agents in that room don't *fully* understand just how powerful these living advantages of life insurance can be. How do I know that? Myriad reasons. The looks on their faces. The '"No way's"' that escape their lips. But the most significant way I know this is due to the number of agents who come up to me after a workshop and say, "You know Patrick, I've been in this business 30 years, and this is the first time I've ever *fully* understood the power of life insurance. I've been missing the boat."

A couple of years back, I asked a veteran of the industry to help me out by role-playing a client as I explained the power of some of these other advantages. At one point in the dialogue, I asked her a question, and she sat there blankly, silently, for an awkward length of time.

Her brother, who was sitting next to her, gave her a little nudge. She looked up, with a look of despondency on her face, and said, "I've been in this business 11 years, and I am just kicking myself that I haven't taken advantage of this. I had no idea how powerful this was. Shame on me!"

Powerful stuff.

So, if the professionals who make their living in this industry don't fully understand the power of the concept, do you think the semi-educated media personalities understand it?

It's important to remember this: Television and radio personalities' primary objectives are to do one thing – entertain. Their show lives or dies based solely upon the number of viewers or listeners who tune in. They are primarily entertainers; they just happen to entertain in the financial space.

Most of these folks are not the financial know-it-alls they appear to be; rather, they tend to know a little about a lot of areas, allowing them to sound financially intelligent, but in reality, making them quite dangerous.

Please don't misinterpret what I'm saying. I'm sure most of them are principled people, with good intentions; it's just that they *don't know what they don't know.*

One of my favorite things to say to an individual is this, "Don't take my word for it. Let the numbers speak for themselves."

I encourage you to do the same. Be objective. Dig in. Run the numbers. And when you do, I think they might surprise you.

Chapter 8

A Story About Tom

I'd like for you to meet Tom. Today is November 20, 2007, and it is Tom's 64th birthday. Tom is eagerly looking forward to retiring next year after more than 30 productive years with his company.

During Tom's working years, he has ridden the ups and downs of the stock market. But he now feels very good about the $2.5-million war-chest he has been able to pile up in his company's 401(k) plan, largely due to the fact that the S&P 500 just hit its all-time high of 1565.15 on October 9, 2007, just a few short weeks before his birthday. *What a great birthday present*, he thinks one morning in late November as he wakes up to the smell of his morning coffee brewing down the hall.

He puts on his sweats, saunters to the kitchen, grabs the morning paper off the front porch and takes his first sip of the morning brew.

Perfect! He thinks. *The market is up. My health is great. And retirement is just around the corner.*

His mind wanders ahead one year to that special point in life he and Julie have been eagerly looking forward to, when he finally has the time and money to pursue some of the interests he's delayed for so long. He and Julie plan to visit Europe, spend time with the grandkids, and certainly enjoy more time together.

It's only one year away, he thinks. *I can hardly wait.*

His morning coffee is sweetened by the taste of what's to come.

The year passes quickly, and Tom is now just a couple of short months away from his long-awaited day. As a matter of fact, he decided he was going to give himself the ultimate birthday present and retire exactly *on* his 65th birthday, November 20, 2008. What a gift that will be.

Today however, as Tom walks into the office on this sunny September morning, there is a different buzz in the air. Things seem just a bit off.

He catches a co-worker passing by and asks, "What's all the ruckus?"

"Haven't you heard?" he says. "The market's been tanking. The entire financial system is on the verge of meltdown."

"Seriously? I didn't have time for the news this morning."

Tom turns toward his computer and signs on to take a look for himself. *Whoa! How can this be?* He wonders.

Tom quickly pulls up his 401(k) account online but he can't get any updated information because it won't be available until after the close of the stock market. *If these percentages are right and my 401(k) follows suit, then I could have lost 9 percent of my life savings in one day!*

He sits there sweating and stewing, sick to his stomach.

It was a long day. A very long day. But finally the stock market closes and he is able to see the damage to his own account.

"Oh no!" he mutters audibly. "No! No! No! This is disaster!"

Tom sits there, numb. On Friday September 26, 2008, three days ago, his 401(k) account value was $2.2 million, down a little from last year's high, but still enough for his pending retirement. Now on Monday, just three days later, it shows his account has lost $210,000 in one trading day.

He quickly picks up the phone to call his best friend, who is also a local stockbroker. "Barry, this is Tom. What's happening? I've just lost nearly 10 percent of my entire 401(k) in one day! What should I do?"

Barry, always the voice of reassurance, does his best to calm Tom down, to soothe his frayed nerves.

"Tom, I know. It was a bad day. But remember, the markets have bad days. It's part of the ride. The nice thing is that markets bounce. Look at history. There have been some terrible years in the past, but the market pushes through those and moves on to higher levels. You just have to relax, hold on, and try not to look too closely at the daily numbers. This will pass. Don't worry."

Don't worry? Tom thinks. *How am I supposed to not worry? I retire in two months and my retirement account is going the wrong direction.*

However, to mask his deep concern, Tom simply says, "Thanks buddy. I'm not sure I'll be able to 'not worry,' but I always appreciate your perspective."

As Tom hangs up the phone, his mood improves slightly as he tries to keep his worst fears at bay. And sure enough, Barry's words once again appear prophetic, because the next day the market does rebound, returning more than half of what Tom had lost the day before.

I'm sure Barry is right. I just need to let the market do its thing and forget about it.

So that's exactly what Tom does, at least for the next two weeks. He goes about his daily life, pushing aside his desire to watch the daily gyrations of the market. But at the end of the day on Friday, October 7, he can't stand the suspense any longer and just has to take a peek. He logs on to view his 401(k) account, Barry's reassuring words echoing in his mind, expecting to see the balance hovering once again around $2.2 million, but instead his ending balance shows $1,520,000.

There must be some mistake. This can't be my account! But after double-checking his online statement he realizes there *is* no mistake. *Where is all my money? I've just lost* ***another*** *20 percent! What am I going to do?*

Quickly Tom signs onto the Web to see what the actual market has done. Sure enough, the S&P 500 has dropped another 20 percent in the last two weeks and now sits at 899.22.

"So much for Barry's future as a prophet," he mutters under his breath as he sits in stunned panic. Tom wants to call Barry again, but the phone is just too heavy. He can't lift it out of its cradle. *Maybe on Monday,* he thinks.

Monday morning, before he can focus on work, he digs deep to find the strength to call Barry, once again hoping for his best friend's reassuring wisdom.

"Hey buddy, it's me. I'm not doing so well, as you might imagine. I took your advice a couple of weeks ago and stopped watching the market, but on Friday I couldn't help but look. I'm sure you know where this conversation is going; it isn't good. Actually, disaster is more appropriate.

My account has gone down a full $1 million in the last 12 months. What should I do?"

"Tom, I wish I could tell you 'Don't worry, this will pass,' but honestly I don't know. No one does. This is new territory for us all."

"Barry, what are you saying? This market might not come back?"

"No, I'm not saying that. I'm just saying that no one knows. But yes, that is always a possibility."

"But didn't you just tell me to hold on, ride it out, hang in there? Now you're telling me you don't know. That's not real comforting."

"Man, I wish I could tell you more. The truth of the matter is that no one knows where this is headed. No one has *ever* known. All we have is history as a guide, and history says to just hang on and ride out the storm. That's all I've got."

"What if I don't *want* to sit passively and ride out the storm? What other options do I have?"

"Certainly you could re-allocate your money. Move it out of the market and into something safe. The problem with that, though, is if the market *does* turn, you will miss out on regaining some of your losses. It's a tough call. I honestly don't know what to tell you," Barry says.

"Thanks for the honesty buddy. I don't particularly like it, but I do appreciate it. I just wish there was something more I could do."

"I know. Me too."

Tom hangs up the phone and stares at his computer screen. *Just six weeks until I retire and my life savings is going up in smoke.*

After thinking about his options, Tom decides to let it ride. He hates the idea of having lost so much money, but he fears missing out on a possible bounce even more.

He crosses his fingers, knocks on wood, and shuts his computer down for the night, feeling a lot more like he's leaving a Vegas roulette table than the desk in his office. *Have I been gambling or investing?* he wonders, as he walks toward his car in the company lot.

November 20, 2008, arrives. It's Tom's 65th birthday and the last working day of his career. The excitement he expected to feel has been extinguished by the market's continued sputtering. He does his best to stay positive, but he's finding it extremely difficult.

By the end of the day, the thin thread of optimism that did exist has snapped completely, leaving behind sheer and utter panic. Today, on Tom's last working day, the day he so eagerly looked forward to, the market ended at a new low. The S&P 500 closed at 752.44, 52 percent *below* it's October 9, 2007, high, the lowest point it has closed in 11½ years. Tom can't believe it. The promise of time, travel, and leisure has evaporated. Of course he and Julie will still survive. He knows there could be much worse losses in life, but it will be a much different existence than the one he envisioned just 13 months ago. That flourishing account that once stood proudly at $2.5 million now squats humbly at $1.2 million.

More than half of what Tom spent the last 30 years accumulating has been wiped out in 13 short months.

He feels sick. He sits stunned. And he does the only thing he can think to do. He picks up the phone at his desk for the very last time, calls the benefits department, and reallocates all of his money to a money market fund, before it *all* evaporates. Although he will earn less than 1 percent interest on his money with this allocation, at least it is safe. He has reached his maximum pain threshold and needs to get out of the market for his own health or he might not live to see a very long retirement.

As he thinks back, all he remembers anyone talking about during his saving years is the amount of taxes he would supposedly save by putting his money into the company 401(k); yet, no one ever talked to him about the market risk involved. *How is that possible?*

What is going to make Tom sicker, if that is even possible, is that the day *after* he moves his money to safety, the market begins to recover. But because of Tom's need for safety and peace of mind, he misses the big bounce. He just couldn't handle the risk of losing any more money.

The other surprise he has yet to discover is that all of those taxes he thought he was saving by contributing to his 401(k) during his working years were not really "saved" at all; they were simply delayed. So not only does his account stand at 48 percent of its value from last year due to market declines, but he *still has to pay tax on every dollar he withdraws from that account.*

Oh boy! Tom is in for a big surprise.

* The numbers and values in this chapter are real. On October 9, 2007 the S&P 500 hit its all-time high of 1565.15. The following year, on November 20, 2008 it hit an 11½ year low, closing at 752.44. If a retirement account had followed the percent of gain and loss that the S&P 500 experienced during that time, its losses would reflect what Tom experienced.

Chapter 9

Is it Really Tax-Free?

So, let's look at a different option, an option that will not only provide protection against negative stock market returns, as outlined earlier in this book, but one that can also free an individual from the big tax surprise that is still in store for our friend Tom.

It is important that all individuals understand that, by definition, a life insurance policy is *a tax-deferred* vehicle. It is *not* a tax-free vehicle. In other words, the cash value within a Universal Life policy *grows* without being taxed, but if this money is simply *withdrawn,* then all the *gains* realized within the policy (the amount above the total premiums paid) *will* be taxed, and taxed as income, not capital gains. Ouch!

However, there *is* another way to tap into the cash value inside your policy – a way that *doesn't* depend on withdrawals. A way that allows you tax-free access. And this method is called the Policy Loan Provision.

Now, don't let the word loan scare you. Once you understand it, I think you're going to feel very comfortable. It's one of the most ingenious creations in the history of finance. And you can use it to your full advantage ... *if* you're one of the few who understand it.

While I explain in detail how the Policy Loan Provision works in my first book, *Tax-Free Retirement*, it bears repeating here for two reasons. The obvious first reason is that you may not have read my first book (shame on you); the second reason is that it is too significant *not* to repeat. If you understand this one provision, you will begin to see its tremendous power. So let me explain.

Let's say you are going to borrow money to buy a new car. Is the *loan* you receive from the bank or credit union taxed? No. The *car* may be taxed (due to state sales tax), but the *loan* is not taxed. Right? *Loans* are not taxed; *items* are taxed.

So life insurance companies, in their brilliant ingenuity, created a contractual policy feature that allows the policy owner to have access to tax-free money by using their life insurance cash value as collateral. This feature enables the owner to avoid any tax on the money received, because it is just a loan from a financial institution, not a withdrawal.

Here's how it works ...

A policy owner can always take a tax-free withdrawal up to the total premiums paid into the policy, subject to surrender charges, because the first money allowed to come out of a life insurance policy is simply a return of the owner's total premium payments, which have already been taxed prior to being put into the policy. However, if an individual wants to withdraw money above the total amount of premiums paid (again, always subject to any surrender charges) then a withdrawal of this gain *would be taxed*. It would be taxed as income, because the policy owner would now be withdrawing money which has not yet been taxed.

But luckily, the owner has *another* option, and this is where the Policy Loan Provision comes into play.

Life insurance companies allow a client to take a loan ***against*** his cash value, not ***from*** his cash value. This is a *very important distinction.* The money is not coming *from* the cash value, but is a loan *against* it. The cash value within a client's policy simply acts as collateral for that loan.

Your initial reaction might be, "Ouch, that doesn't sound like a good plan during my retirement years. I don't want to be taking loans." But what if you were charged 0 percent interest *and* did not need to pay the loan back during your lifetime? Would that change the picture? You bet it would.

Here's how this works.

The amount that an individual borrows *does* get charged an interest rate, just like any other loan. For illustration sake lets assume that rate is 4 percent. So the individual is now being charged 4 percent per year on his borrowed money, but that is only half of the story.

When an individual takes out a loan, the life insurance company then essentially removes that same amount of money from his cash value as collateral and puts it into a separate account that also earns 4 percent. So let's do the math. If he is being *charged* 4 percent on his loan but is also *earning* 4 percent on the cash value acting as collateral for this loan, then what is the net loan interest rate essentially being charged? Zero. Does that make sense?

The client is being charged the same rate of interest on his loan that he is earning on the cash value acting as collateral, allowing him to experience a 0 percent *net* interest rate. This is often referred to as the Wash Loan Provision, which is provided to those utilizing the Fixed Loan option. (Please read the special note at the end of this chapter marked with a single asterisk to understand more about this loan option.)

So what does this allow him to do? Through this provision, he is able to continue to access amounts equal to his cash value during his lifetime,** tax-free and interest-free (after a certain number of years.)*** It really doesn't get any better than that.

Yet, the good news doesn't stop there. Since the money is distributed as a loan, it doesn't show up on his annual tax return. As far as the IRS is concerned, it's invisible money that he gets to use during his lifetime, tax-free.

The last component I need to explain in order for you to understand how this all fits together is how the life insurance death benefit is treated from a tax standpoint, because it is the unique tax treatment of the death benefit that makes this whole strategy work. Without the death benefit, this strategy would not exist.

Death benefit proceeds are income-tax free. They are not estate-tax free without creating special trusts, but they are income-tax free. So when a policy owner dies, his tax-free and interest-free loan received during his lifetime is paid off with the income-tax-free death benefit. And once this loan is paid off, what's left over gets paid to his beneficiary, also income-tax free.

Incredible! Income-tax-free dollars while you're living and income-tax-free dollars distributed to whomever you choose upon your death.

Right now you might be asking yourself two questions. The first is, "Okay, what's the catch?"

To that question I can only tell you there really isn't any catch. There is a caution that I will cover in a minute, but there is no catch. As long as you understand that you are buying life insurance, then there really isn't any catch. Most people need the life insurance protection anyway, so purchasing it in this manner is a great way to get the life insurance protection they need and some potential tax advantages they didn't know existed.

The second question you may be asking yourself is, "Why isn't everyone doing this?"

I believe the first reason more individuals aren't utilizing this strategy is because they simply don't know about it. It has been hidden, a mystery, but a mystery I'm hoping to reveal to all individuals in America.

The second likely reason why everyone isn't doing this is because it is not *for* everybody. Though it is *open* to everybody who can qualify for and needs life insurance, it is often best suited for those who earn a relatively large income or for individuals who want to save more each year than a Roth IRA will allow.

Previously I mentioned that there is a caution that needs to be well heeded. That caution is simply this: Since it is the income-tax-free death benefit that makes this entire strategy work, *it is **imperative** that the policy stays in force until the insured's death*. That may sound pretty basic, but it is too important to gloss over. The reason that the policy *must stay in force* is that if the policy cancels for any reason, then all of the gain that has been taken as a tax-free loan will suddenly become taxable, and that is one tax bill you never want to see!

So, how do you make sure the policy stays in force? Simple. First, don't take out too much money. Also, when your agent runs an income illustration, make sure that he or she runs it all the way to age 120 (formerly 100.) Don't let someone try to show you better income projections by running them to only age 90 or 95. Do I think most individuals are going to live to age 120? No. But running the income stream all the way out to the end of the policy, which is now 120 with most top life insurance carriers, is just another way to be conservative with your projections.

Second, review your policy annually with the person who sold it to you. If your policy is returning less than the illustration predicted, take out less money for a while until it catches up.

As a side note, make sure you buy this policy from a top-rated life insurance company, as well as from an agent who fully understands how this strategy works. You need the personal assistance of a qualified individual who will be able to walk you through the best distribution strategy possible.

Really, there is nothing to be scared of. You just need to show caution and discernment as you set up a successful distribution plan for your future.

* The type of loan described in this chapter is the Fixed Loan, sometimes referred to as a Wash Loan. There is another type of loan called the Variable Loan, which does *NOT* operate in the way described in this book. And while the illustrations shown using the Variable Loan often look better on paper than a Fixed Loan, the Variable Loan forces the consumer to take on both significant interest-rate and market risk in the future, once loans have been taken from the policy. The Fixed Loan is much safer, because it is contractually guaranteed – the Variable Loan is not. My suggestion, for caution's sake, is to utilize the Fixed Loan for illustration purposes.

** When an individual takes money from his or her policy in the form of either a withdrawal or a loan, both reduce the cash value of the life insurance policy and potentially the death benefit as well. All of these reductions are factored into and represented by the illustration, so no further calculations are necessary by the client. However, an individual will want to make sure, as with all financial products, that he or she doesn't take out too much money, too early, as this could cause the policy to lapse. (Again, another reason to work with someone who can expertly guide you though this process in a safe and effective manner.)

*** While life insurance companies generally allow policy owners to take a very low interest rate loan against their cash value as soon as cash value is available, the ability to participate in the Wash Loan provision, allowing a net 0 percent interest rate, usually occurs 10 or more years after the policy is put in force, depending on the company. Each company has different requirements, so it is important that you know your policy's provisions.

Note: The reason I placed these three comments as notes at the end of this chapter, instead of imbedding them within the chapter, was simply so they would not distract the flow of the overall explanation.

Chapter 10

Never Lose Money

With Indexed Universal Life Insurance, you will ***never*** lose money due to a market decline … ever! How good is that?

(End of chapter. Really!)

Chapter 11

Up, Up and Away

In regard to the stock market, I'm convinced of one thing. Nobody, and I mean *nobody*, knows where it's headed in the future. No one. Not your stockbroker. Not your stockbroker's analysts. Not the chairman of the Fed or the secretary of the treasury. And certainly not the president of the United States or the leader of any other country, for that matter.

No one knows. It's just that simple.

Let me give you one very sage piece of advice. If anyone tells you he knows what the stock market is going to do over the next set of months or years, run! And run quickly. It will save you a lot of money.

With that said, many people have guesses, including me, but that's all they are, guesses. And if I was forced to describe, in one word, what I believe the next 10 years might look like, that one word would be *choppy*. The market could go up. The market could go down. My guess is that we are likely to see a lot of both.

But again, I don't know, and neither does anyone else.

The more important question is: What do *you* think the

stock market is going to do over the next decade? If you don't have a clue, welcome to the club. However, there are only three possibilities.

1. The market goes up
2. The market goes down
3. The market goes sideways

As I said, if I were betting, I'd place my money on Door No. 3, but let's take a look at all three possibilities.

Possibility No. 1: The Market Goes Up

If you knew without a shadow of doubt that the market was going to be higher in the future than it is today, what would you do? Easy, right? You'd get as much money into it, right now, as you possibly could. Why? Because if it's going up, that means more money.

But, do we know that the market is going to go up? Of course not.

So, without the certainty of knowing that the market is going up, the prospect of pumping all of your money into it is as perilous as swimming down the Amazon River in a Speedo with a T-bone steak tied to each ankle.

Possibility No. 2: The Market Goes Down

Now, if you knew the market was going to be lower in the future, what would you do? That, too, is hardly a tough question.

You would get out. Abandon ship. Avoid it completely.

You might hold cash; you might buy gold; you might invest in real estate; you'd do something, anything, but you would *not* put your money in the market because to do so would be certain loss.

Possibility No. 3: The Market Goes Sideways

Even novice investors recognize that markets don't just go up and just don't go down. They also travel sideways, neither up nor down, along their meandering course to who-knows-where.

Let's take a look at how both the general stock market and an Indexed Universal Life Policy's cash value would perform in a long-term choppy (sideways) market.

For this hypothetical example, let's pretend each year alternated between a 10-percent gain and a 10-percent loss. Could this really happen? No, at least not with exact repetition; however, this will serve as a powerful teaching tool.

In this hypothetical example, the graph for those market returns would look like figure 11.1 below.

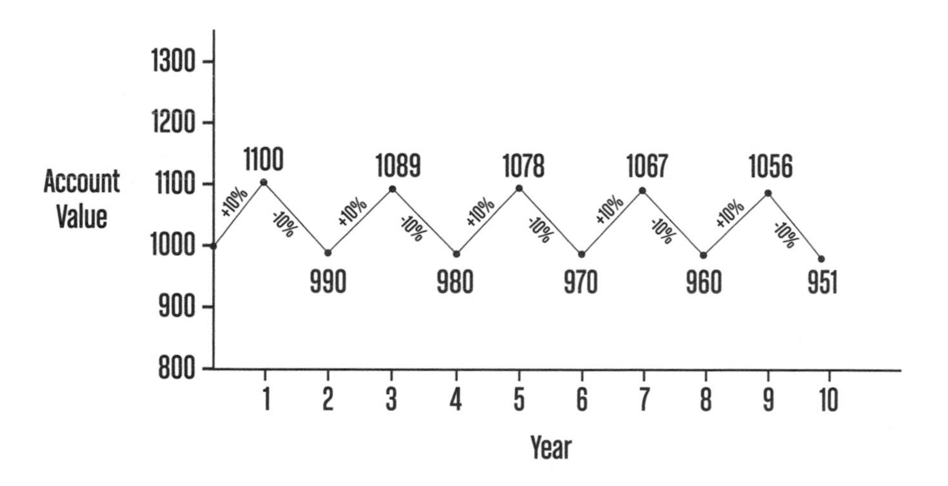

Figure 11.1

Here's what's interesting. If an account performed in this manner, with a 10-percent gain in year one, a 10-percent loss in year two, and then alternated back and forth that way for 10 years, its average return at the end of those 10 years would be zero. However, the actual return would be a negative 4.9 percent. Yes, it would have lost money. An account that started with $1,000 at the beginning of this 10-year period but experienced alternating years of 10-percent gain and 10-percent loss, would end up with an account value of only $950.99. Crazy, isn't it?

How can the same gain and same loss, alternating each year for 10 years, result in *less* money than an investor began with? If the average return on this account is 0 percent, doesn't that mean it will end at its beginning value of $1,000 at the end of that roller coaster ride? Nope. (Remember: The *average* return and the *actual* return will *never* equal one another if any negative numbers have to be factored into the equation.) Here's how the actual results would look, year by year:

END OF YEAR	GAIN OR LOSS	VALUE OF ACCOUNT
1	10%	$1,100.00
2	(-10%)	$990.00
3	10%	$1,089.00
4	(-10%)	$980.10
5	10%	$1,078.11
6	(-10%)	$970.30
7	10%	$1,067.33
8	(-10%)	$960.60
9	10%	$1,056.66
10	(-10%)	$950.99

Figure 11.2

As you can see, the account continues to lose ground each and every two-year period. Not only would that individual not see a single penny of gain, he would have actually experienced a 5-percent loss. He would have been better off sticking that $1,000 into a coffee can and burying it in his back yard.

Now let's see how this same market would look if we overlaid upon it the two principles that are offered by the Indexed strategy – no losses in negative market years, and capturing (and protecting) each positive year's gain. The difference is shocking. Here are the numbers:

END OF YEAR	GAIN OR LOSS	VALUE OF ACCOUNT
1	10%	$1,100.00
2	0%	$1,100.00
3	10%	$1,210.00
4	0%	$1,210.00
5	10%	$1,331.00
6	0%	$1,331.00
7	10%	$1,464.10
8	0%	$1,464.10
9	10%	$1,610.51
10	0%	$1,610.51

Figure 11.3

Wow! This is the same market but radically different results.

The percent of growth in the up years was the same in both scenarios – 10 percent; the only difference between these two charts is the fact that the Indexed Strategy never experienced a negative return. Its worst year was zero. And even though it only had five out of 10 years of gain, that initial $1,000 investment would have grown to $1,610.51 at the end of 10 years – a 61-percent *gain* in a market that had an average return of 0 percent, and a real return (loss) of -4.9 percent.

Do you see how powerful the Indexed strategy can be even in a choppy or sideways market? Why? Because in the year that the general market went down, the Indexed strategy stayed flat – it didn't lose value. Therefore, when the stock market grew the following year, the Indexed strategy was able to grow from the previous year's high-water mark; it didn't have to make up any losses just to get you back to even, because it never had any losses. Let that sink in. Really sink in. It's revolutionary.

To help you picture what this scenario looks like graphically, see figure 11.4 across:

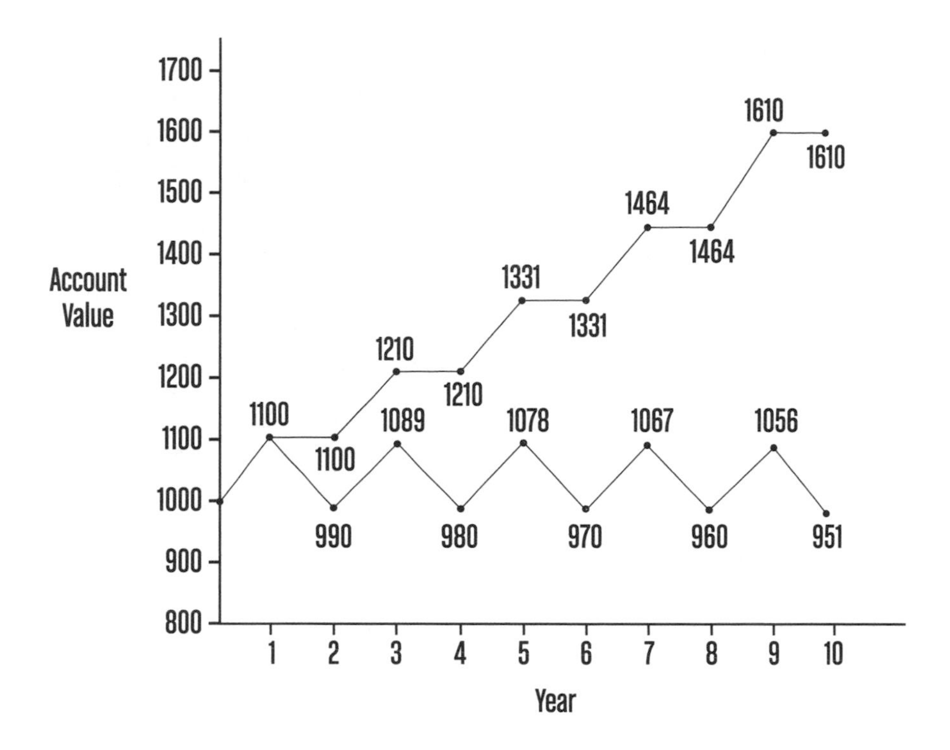

Figure 11.4

And don't let this fact slip by you; in this hypothetical example above, after 10 years, there would be 69.35 percent *more money* in the Indexed strategy than in a non-Indexed strategy. So, not only does this product offer a safety net against loss, but it also provides the opportunity for remarkable growth, even in choppy and volatile markets.

Note: This scenario above does not include any fees, costs, management expenses, or any other type of sales charge of any particular product on either side of the comparison. Rather, it is simply a look at how the different *strategies* would perform in this type of market. The only way to evaluate the actual costs, expenses, and opportunities available to you is to meet with a financial professional, who can run the various options side by side, so you can evaluate each and make the best decision for your financial future.

Chapter 12

How Can They Do That?

Financial professionals often ask me the same question you likely have running through your brain at this very moment: "How can any company let you share in stock market gains without making you participate in the losses as well?" It just seems too good to be true; but fortunately, it's not. It's very real and very possible.

If you are familiar with the many different terms in the financial universe then you have likely heard of a financial tool called an "option." However, you may not know what an option actually is or how it works.

An option is simply a tool that allows a person to profit from the *direction* of a market. If a person owns an option, he or she doesn't own any particular underlying stock. Rather, the owner is simply betting on (and will make a profit or loss from) the *direction* of a market movement.

There are two basic types of options: Puts and Calls.

Those who own a *Put Option* will make a profit when a market goes *down*. Those who own a *Call Option* will make a profit when a market goes *up*. In its basic form, it really is that simple.

When a client purchases an Indexed UL, a premium is charged based on the amount of death benefit chosen. The higher the death benefit, the higher the premium. However, this premium covers more than just the cost of insurance. It also pays for all of the other policy and administrative fees as well. In this particular type of policy, a small percentage of the premium also goes to purchase an option – a Call Option to be exact. And it is this Call Option that allows the life insurance company to provide a market-like return, up to a specified cap, without actually being invested in the market at all.

I'm sure you're asking yourself, "How can a company give you a market-like return without actually being invested in the market?" Here's how.

When you pay the premium on your Indexed UL, the life insurance company invests the vast majority of that money (after expenses) in a safe and predictable bond portfolio. For illustration sake, let's assume that the amount is 95 percent of the investable premium available. Since 95 percent of this money is invested in bonds, the life insurance company is able to determine with near certainty at what point in the future that 95 percent will grow back to the full 100 percent with which it started. It's safe. It's predictable. And it carries no market risk.

However, since only 95 percent of the investable premium is used to purchase bonds, there is still 5 percent available to use elsewhere. And it is this 5 percent that is used to buy Call Options on the market that the Indexed UL is tracking. And since Call Options exponentially increase in value when a particular market goes up, this increase in value allows the insurance company to pass on those gains in the form of market-like returns, when the markets have a positive year.

Simply put, bonds provide the downside protection guarantee and Call Options provide the upside growth potential.

Does this make sense? I hope so. If nothing else, just know that these returns and guarantees are not some mystical leap of faith, but rather a predictable set of calculations prepared by some of the world's most gifted mathematicians.

Chapter 13

What if Tax Laws Change?

You've heard it said that there are only two guarantees in life: death and taxes. I'd like to add a third to that list – tax law *changes*.

Unfortunately, all of our crystal balls perform with the same accuracy. When we stare into them, all we'll see is a dark, murky cloud. It's the land of the unknown. Just as no one knows what the stock market will do in the future, neither does anyone know what tax laws will do. The only certainty is change.

Regardless of what happens, the one thing I can guarantee is this – taxes in the future will look different than they do today. That's been our history and will certainly continue to be so. Change after change after change.

Here's a graph that shows the history of the top marginal tax bracket in the United States since just after 1910:

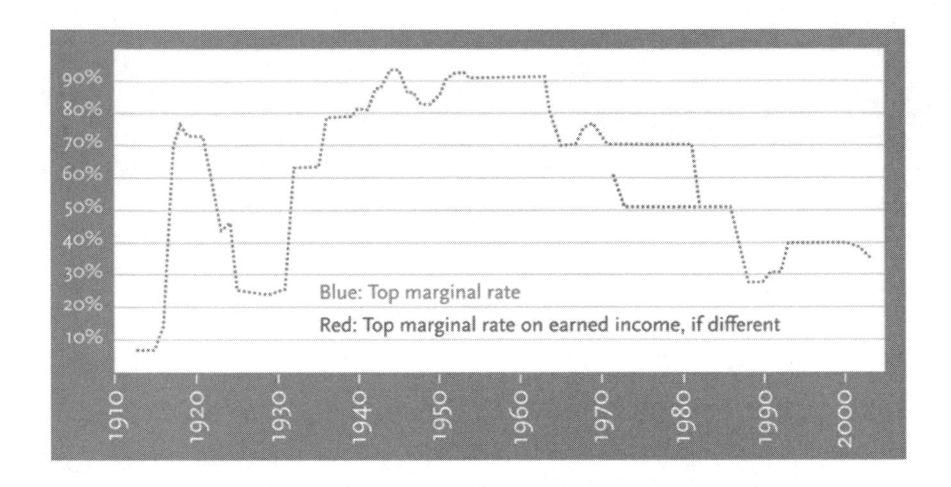

Figure 12.1

(truthandpolitics.org, referencing IRS Statistics of Income Bulletin Pub 1136)[12]

See what I mean? No consistency.

Take a moment to study the graph. Let it sink in. Look at those years during the '40s, '50s, and '60s. Do you see what occurred? The top marginal tax bracket during those decades spent most of its time above 90 percent. Shocking! Utterly outrageous! (I encourage you to look at the actual top marginal tax rate, year by year, listed in the Appendix.)

In 2011, our top marginal tax bracket is 35 percent. High-income earners just dodged a bullet because top marginal tax rates were scheduled to go to 39.6 percent. But a little political shake-up put that on hold, at least for a couple of years. Yet, as bad as those rates feel, they pale in comparison to what people experienced just a few decades ago. As a matter of fact, as you look at this graph above, you see that tax rates are near historic lows.

On the other hand, our spending as a nation has grown exponentially. We are now incurring annual deficits the size of what was recently our entire national debt.

Does that seem like a disconnect? It should. Do you really think that dichotomy can last forever?

Regardless of what tax rates do in the future, you can see from our history that rarely are they static. We can count on change and lots of it.

So, sticking with history, let's take a look back at how the tax treatment of life insurance contracts has been affected by our ever-changing tax law. And to do that, I'm going to tell you a story.

Back in the early 1980s, individuals were able to buy very small Universal Life policies and stick hundreds of thousands of dollars into them. There was virtually no limit as to how much an individual could contribute. The IRS eventually took a look at this and decided this hardly resembled life insurance at all; rather, the agency felt it was simply a way for an individual to shelter an unlimited amount of money from future taxation.

So, to combat this, a set of laws was created requiring a defined relationship between the amount of money an individual could put into a policy and the amount of death benefit that needed to be purchased. Under this new law, individuals could no longer put an unlimited amount of money into their policy.

However – and this is the big *however* – the tax-law change applied *only* to new policies that were issued *from that date forward.* The policies that were in force prior to that tax-law change were grandfathered in under the old set of tax laws. In other words, those early policies were *still* able to take advantage of the original set of laws.

So, if history repeats itself, and the government treats future tax-law changes regarding life insurance as they have previously, more than likely you will be able to operate under the laws in force when the policy was issued. Of course, there is no guarantee here; however, a pretty strong precedent has been set.

Also, it is important to remember that a life insurance policy is a contract – a contract that was entered into under a certain set of rules. I think the government would have a big fight on its hands if it tried to change the terms of a contract retroactively.

So what does this mean for you? While we have no idea what tax laws will be in the future, we *do* know what they are right now. And right now, you are able to grow the cash value inside of your Universal Life policy tax-deferred and then access this cash value tax-free, utilizing the Policy Loan Provision. You might want to consider getting on this train before it leaves the station! Because once it leaves, it's likely gone.

Chapter 14

The Ideal Answer

If I had started out this book and, in the first few chapters, told you there was a product that would ...

1. Allow you to draw income in retirement tax-free
2. Receive market-like returns without any market risk
3. Never take a market loss
4. Allow you access to your money at any age
5. Give you an option to continue to make your savings contributions if you become disabled
6. Provide a large, income-tax-free, lump sum payment to your family if you died prematurely
7. Remain protected against judgments and lawsuits (in many states)

... I'm sure you would have laughed, written me off as a nut job, and thrown this book into the closest recycle bin.

All of us are taught from an early age to doubt something that seems too good to be true. And generally that is sound advice. It has saved me from many mistakes. But there *are* times when something really *is* that good, and this is one of those times.

Again, as I said earlier, don't just take my word for it, let the numbers speak for themselves. And the best way to do that is to have a personal consultation with a qualified, knowledgeable, financial consultant who understands exactly how this product works – very likely the person who gave you this book.

I had a person tell me once that if all those features above were true, then his question was not *should* he do this, but rather, *how much* and *how soon.*

Chapter 15

The Best-Kept Secret

This is a chapter I've been eager to write. (Chomping at the bit, really.) You are going to find its practical uses remarkably simple, but profoundly revolutionary. Again, this won't be a fit for every person who reads this book, but for those it does, it will open up possibilities never imagined.

In my opinion, the *perfect* candidate for this strategy is the business owner. There are certainly other applications, such as a person who might receive a future inheritance, a person who may sell a piece of investment property down the road, or anyone who will receive any type of future lump sum of money. However, even though all of the above are possible candidates who could benefit from this concept, my specific focus for this chapter will be why this concept is such a tremendous gift distinctly for the business owner.

In my workshops I love to ask this question. "What percent of business owners do you think want to sell their business someday?"

The responses shouted are always the same.

"All!"

"100 percent!"

"Everyone!"

Granted, while I think the answer *is* "most" of them, "all" might be a tad aggressive. So my reply to the group is, "Who knows? Let's just say it's somewhere on the corner of 'Most & All'."

But here's the absurd thing. While most business owners *do* plan to sell their business someday, few, if any, have ever paused long enough to think about *where* they will invest the proceeds from that sale. They've thought about *how much* they hope to make and *what age* they might sell it, but they've never thought about the most important part of the sale – *where* they are going to put those future funds someday.

Why is this such a critical question? Because without planning for that event early, the business owner's options will be severely limited. Here's why.

Let's assume the business owner sells his business, pays the capital gains tax that is due, and now has $1 million of cash he would like to put somewhere for future use. What typical options are usually considered?

- Stocks
- Bonds
- Mutual Funds
- Certificates of Deposit

But what if the business owner desires two additional characteristics as well?

- Safety, *and*
- High Growth Potential

How many of those original four options provide both safety *AND* high growth potential? If you said, "None," you'd be correct. Each item on that original list provides either safety *OR* high growth potential, but none of them provide both. It's virtually unheard of in the marketplace.

Okay, let's make the air even thinner and add three more qualifying factors to the list:

- Tax-deferred growth
- Tax-free access during his lifetime, and
- An income-tax free benefit that will pass to his heirs at death

Any potential candidates now on your list? Yeah, I thought so. What product can provide ***all*** of those features and still accept an incredibly large lump-sum of money? (With the proper advanced planning, of course.)

Are Tax-Qualified Plans an option? Not even close! While Tax-Qualified Plans allow workers to make annual deposits up to the contribution limit of the plan, they have no ability to receive a large deposit in one lump sum.

It's important you understand this.

Just for illustration sake, let's assume a Tax-Qualified Plan allowed an annual deposit of $49,000 in the current year. And let's also assume that the plan participant contributed $0 into that plan in that particular year.

Question. How much of that $49,000 contribution limit can be carried over to next year if it is not utilized? In other words, if the individual contributes $0 in 2011, can he contribute twice that amount, $98,000, in 2012? ($49,000 for 2012 *plus* the $49,000 missed in 2011.) No. A big, fat, definitive "No!"

Tax-Qualified Plans work on a "use-it-or-lose-it" proposition each and every year. There is no carry-over provision.

So it's clear, Tax-Qualified Plans are not an option for a

future, large, single deposit that a business owner may desire to make from the sale of his or her business.

Now the business owner, who has $1 million to invest, could put this money into the bank, a credit union, CDs, mutual funds, stocks or bonds. But, each and every one of these options is taxable, either annually or at some time in the future.

Ask yourself, where can you put a lump sum of $1 million that has *any* tax-advantaged growth possibilities? If you come up blank, don't feel badly. When I ask that question to a room full of financial advisors, I have yet, even once, to have any individual give a single answer. The room remains completely quiet.

I'm aware of only one option available that fits all these criteria: Indexed Universal Life. Okay, you probably saw that coming. Sorry, but once you really understand it, fully comprehend it, you'll be amazed at the advantage it can provide. Here's how this strategy works.

One of the nice features of Indexed Universal Life insurance is that it allows an individual the benefit of a flexible premium. That means the individual has a flexible range of premium payment options between a minimum amount the life insurance company *requires* and a maximum amount that the IRS *allows*.

The minimum premium is simply the amount the issuing life insurance company charges in order for the client to be able to purchase a particular policy. Hypothetically, let's say that a 35-year-old male, earning $150,000 a year, buys a $1 million IUL policy. The minimum premium required by the life insurance company might be in the neighborhood of $800 per month. However, there is another amount the client needs to take into consideration, a much more exciting amount. This amount represents the *maximum* premium that the IRS *allows* an individual to be able to put into a policy without creating what is called a Modified Endowment Contract – which, in simple terms, essentially takes away most of the beneficial tax advantages. (And as I like to say, "In my experience, any time the IRS limits what you can put into something, it's usually because it's a pretty good deal.") In this hypothetical example, let's assume that the most this 35-year-old could put in (without creating a MEC) is $40,000 per year. So, in our example, this young business owner could contribute anywhere between $10,000 and $40,000 per year.

Let me ask you a question. What do *all* businesses demand in the early years? If you said "cash," you'd be correct. Every young business needs capital. Cash flow is king. New businesses are almost *always* starving for cash.

So while we've talked about how powerful it might be for an individual to put the maximum premium into this type of life insurance policy in order to benefit from a large tax-free cash flow in the future, most business owners are just not in a position to be able to make the maximum contribution, at least in the early years. Does that make this life insurance strategy a poor option for the small business owner who can't contribute near the maximum amount allowed?

Absolutely not! As a matter of fact, it's just the contrary. Here's where this gets really good. Let's look at how this particular type of life insurance policy can provide a completely different option to the business owner, an option that frankly could revolutionize his retirement years and beyond.

Let's say this young business owner, who needs a certain amount of death benefit to protect his family and pay off his business debts, is not able to contribute the maximum premium of $40,000 that his policy would allow, but that he could indeed contribute the $10,000 minimum premium that the company requires.

I want to ask you a question. It's not a trick question. If this individual paid an annual premium of $10,000 in the current year, but *could have* put in up to a maximum of $40,000 in that particular year, how much more *could* he have contributed if he had been able? If you said $30,000, you'd be correct. ($40,000 maximum premium minus $10,000 contributed, leaves $30,000 potential premium remaining – there's some tough math for you. Like I said, it wasn't a trick question.)

Now, unlike a Tax-Qualified Plan, which does not carry over any of its unused contribution amount, guess what happens to the $30,000 of potential premium that wasn't contributed into the life insurance policy? It carries over. Do you want to know for how long? Here's the magic – forever! Are the light bulbs beginning to flicker just a little?

Let me paint the full picture. Let's say this 35-year-old business owner planned to sell his business at age 65 – 30 years from today, and that during each of the 30 years between age 35 and 65 he only contributed $10,000 annually to his IUL policy (though he could have contributed up to $40,000 each year.) In other words, he had an additional $30,000 that he *could have* contributed each year that he *didn't* contribute. Here's where it gets really fun. Each year, that $30,000 shortfall carries forward to the next year ... and continues to do so ... forever!

That's right. In year two, this individual could contribute the $40,000 allowed for *the current* year premiums *plus* the additional $30,000 he didn't put into the policy in year one. And that only illustrates the power in just the first two years of the policy. What if we now stretch that same scenario out for the full 30 years? If this individual puts in $30,000 *less* than the maximum contribution amount each year for 30 years, guess what he is able to contribute into the policy in the 31st year? That's right! Most, if not all, of his previously missed premiums. (The reason I say most is that this can vary from company to company. Some products seem to accommodate all the missed premiums, while other accept an amount close to, but a little shy of, the total of the missed premiums. As is always the case, if this is something you are interested in, have your prospective life insurance company run an illustration for your specific situation so you can see well in advance what you can expect. However, for the rest of *this* hypothetical illustration, let's assume that this particular policy will accept all the missed premiums.)

This individual would have created a bucket big enough to allow him to contribute an additional $900,000 ($30,000 additional missed premium per year multiplied by 30 years) in year 31 without negatively affecting his policy. Why? Because an individual can make up most, if not all, of the past premium amounts that were not contributed.

Think about that! Tax-deferred growth, tax-free access, and the ability to pass the money to one's heirs income-tax free.

Where else can you contribute a large, lump sum of money that has *any* tax-advantaged benefit whatsoever? Nowhere! It doesn't exist. It doesn't exist, that is, except for Universal Life Insurance, *but* only if it has been planned well in advance so that it has the capacity to receive it.

And if utilized properly, this is not just a *little* tax-advantage; rather, it is money that can be accessed and passed on income-tax free.

Now do you see why I was so excited to share this chapter with you? If you are a business owner who plans to eventually sell your business, or an individual who might receive a future inheritance or possibly sell some future investment property, you want to plan *now* for that future contribution. You *NEED* to plan now. Why? Because it is *time* that allows that large bucket to be created. This is a perfect strategy for someone who has 20, 30, or 40 years left until he sells his business or receives an inheritance. It's the $30,000 of additional premium he *could have* contributed, multiplied by the number of years that he *didn't contribute* it, that allows this large bucket to be built.

If someone waits until he is two years away from selling his business, then it's not going to be a very large bucket. He or she would only get to carry over two years of past premiums – or $60,000 (for sake of consistent illustration) – instead of 30 years or $900,000.

Does this make sense? I hope so. But just in case, on the next page is a chart that will show you just how these numbers could look.

Age	Year	Current Year Premium Allowed	Premium Contributed	Additional Premium Allowable (example only)
35	1	$40,000	$10,000	$30,000
36	2	$40,000	$10,000	$60,000
37	3	$40,000	$10,000	$90,000
38	4	$40,000	$10,000	$120,000
39	5	$40,000	$10,000	$150,000
40	6	$40,000	$10,000	$180,000
41	7	$40,000	$10,000	$210,000
42	8	$40,000	$10,000	$240,000
43	9	$40,000	$10,000	$270,000
44	10	$40,000	$10,000	$300,000
45	11	$40,000	$10,000	$330,000
46	12	$40,000	$10,000	$360,000
47	13	$40,000	$10,000	$390,000
48	14	$40,000	$10,000	$420,000
49	15	$40,000	$10,000	$450,000
50	16	$40,000	$10,000	$480,000
51	17	$40,000	$10,000	$510,000
52	18	$40,000	$10,000	$540,000
53	19	$40,000	$10,000	$570,000
54	20	$40,000	$10,000	$600,000
55	21	$40,000	$10,000	$630,000
56	22	$40,000	$10,000	$660,000
57	23	$40,000	$10,000	$690,000

58	24	$40,000	$10,000	$720,000
59	25	$40,000	$10,000	$750,000
60	26	$40,000	$10,000	$780,000
61	27	$40,000	$10,000	$810,000
62	28	$40,000	$10,000	$840,000
63	29	$40,000	$10,000	$870,000
64	30	$40,000	$10,000	$900,000

Figure 17.1

Note: Sometimes it's important to spell out the obvious, so please understand that the benefits discussed throughout this entire book, including the concept discussed in this chapter, are based on tax laws *as of the writing of this book*. No one knows what future taxation will be, and it's possible that future tax laws could change or alter this, or any other, strategy. Again, that's why I encourage you to meet with a professional who understands how this product works so you can walk though the maze of current opportunities available to you today.

Chapter 16

The **Other** Option

After my father read an early manuscript of my first book, *Tax-Free Retirement*, he called me on the phone and opened the conversation with 10 simple words, "Patrick, nice job. But is it too late for me?"

I remember being particularly struck by his question. One, because it was so direct. Two, because it *was* unfortunately too late. I couldn't help him, at least in regard to building a tax-free retirement. He could not take advantage of the strategy I had just spent eight years writing about, because all his money had already been accumulated. It was neatly packaged inside Uncle Sam's favorite account – a self-directed IRA – unable to be accessed without paying income tax, because once money is accumulated within a tax-qualified plan, there is simply no way to access it without Uncle Sam taking his cut.

At the time my dad spoke those words, I had no idea just how many people would ask that same question. It has been amazingly common. And this chapter is their answer.

You see, the strategy discussed so far in this book, as well as in my first book, is primarily for those who are currently in the accumulation phase of their lives, but *not* for those who are already retired or who have accumulated most of their retirement resources. Of course, this is not a definitive rule, since every individual's situation is unique; however, it is a fairly safe generalization.

So what about all those individuals who are not in the accumulation phase of their lives any longer? Those who are already in, or near, retirement? Are they left out in the cold, unable to participate in the powerful wealth-building features offered by Indexed Products?

The good news is that they are *not* left out. While the approach will differ from the plan outlined so far in this book, there is another method. A method I call the *Other* Option. A method that will allow them to grow their money without the risk of market loss, even if they've already accumulated all of their retirement money inside of a tax-qualified plan like a 401(k) or IRA.

Think about what I just said. Let that sink in.

If you are an individual that has already accumulated your retirement savings, ***there is a way for you to grow your money without taking any risk of losing a single cent due to stock market volatility.*** That is a combination virtually unheard of for the retiree (or anyone else for that matter), a combination that changes everything. Here's why.

It is common practice for nearly all individuals, once they reach retirement age, to reallocate their portfolio to minimize risk. Why? Simple. They can't sustain a major hit to the value of their portfolios because they have neither the time, nor the current income, to make up those losses. So they trade risk and growth for safety and stagnancy because they don't know of any financial instrument that can provide both growth *and* safety. Not a bad trade, really.

Just ask my father who retired one month before the tech bubble burst. He hadn't taken the opportunity to reallocate his own portfolio – one, because he was busy wrapping up a successful 34-year medical career and two, because it wasn't *his* job anyway. He had supposedly hired someone to do that for him. (Yeah, right!) And what gift did the market give him in the first month of his retirement? A devastating hit to the portfolio he had spent decades building. Much of it vanished in a few short months. Horrific. As a matter of fact, he had to come out of retirement, strap back on the pads for another year like a battered Brett Favre, and try to recover some of those awful losses. Needless to say, it was not a happy way to enter what was supposed to be his golden years.

So, is reallocating a portfolio to safety a good plan for the retiree? On one hand, it can be, but on the other hand, it creates an entirely different problem – the lack of future growth.

When a person gives up risk, he also usually gives up the potential for a higher return, settling instead for a safe option with a very low return. As I was writing this chapter, I thought I would search the Internet to see what CDs are currently yielding. Up came a paid advertisement boasting, "*CD yields up to 2.4 percent.*" That's about as thrilling as a bungee jump off my living room sofa.

So, I clicked on the site and here's what I found. CD rates (and these are good ones) currently range from 0.69 percent for a three-month CD, to 2.37 percent for a five-year CD. Wow! 2.37 percent! That ought to make you rich – if you have like 150 years to live.

But people don't choose this option for its stellar return, but rather because it is safe, and this safety allows them to sleep at night. There comes a time, as the saying goes, when people care more about getting a return *of* their money than they do about getting a return *on* their money.

Here's the problem with the safety model. While it is vitally important to protect your life's savings, every person and every savings account has an enemy chipping away at it 24 hours a day, seven days a week, 365 days a year. And this enemy's name is inflation, and Mr. Inflation is out to erode everything you have worked so hard to accomplish.

You see, the historical inflation rate, alone, will often consume more spending power than the safe portfolio will grow, even if a person is not drawing any money out of it. But that's the other big problem. Once a person hits retirement, he *is* drawing money out of it. So now he faces a double-whammy. The safe portfolio is shrinking every year due to the fact that he is withdrawing money from the account, *and* what is left in the account is also shrinking in purchasing power due to the effects of Mr. Inflation. This is the dreaded death spiral of retirement accounts.

And while people like the prospect of sleeping peacefully at night, knowing their money is not going to lose value due to a market correction, this move to safety births another daunting fear, one just as malignant as market risk – the fear of running out of money! Retirees don't want to outlive their money. And who can blame them? But unfortunately, the disastrous combination of withdrawals and inflation can erode their account faster than a sandbar in a hurricane, making that fear very, very real.

So retirees face the proverbial "Catch 22": If they leave their money in the stock market, they face the possibility of significant losses (remember my dad's experience), but if they move their money to safety, they face the equally real issue of running out of money due to the negative effects of inflation.

What can they do? Is there an answer?

Yes – a powerful one. It's the *Other* Option.

Before I give you all the specifics about this other option, I want to ask you a hypothetical question. Let's pretend you own a house – free and clear, no mortgage. And let's assume the current appraised value of this home is $500,000. Here's the question.

If you owned this $500,000 house free and clear, would you insure it? Would you pay a few hundred dollars a year to make sure that if it burned to the ground, was damaged in a windstorm, or was vandalized by hooligans, it would be repaired or replaced?

Of course you would!

Maybe even asking that question seems ludicrous to you. You might be thinking, *what nut wouldn't pay a few hundred dollars a year to protect that large and valuable asset?*

Really, the thought of owning such a valuable home and leaving it uninsured is preposterous. Most people wouldn't even consider it.

Yet, most Americans do that very thing with an asset that is worth as much or even more than their house – their retirement account! And why do they leave this huge asset uninsured? Simply because they didn't know there was a way they *could* insure it against loss.

What if I told you that you *could* insure your retirement savings against loss *and,* at the same time, participate in some of the annual growth of the stock market *and,* maybe best of all, insure that you will protect all the previous years of growth as well?

Guess what? You can. That financial tool *does* exist. It's

called an Indexed Annuity. And the great thing about an annuity is that you *can* transfer all your tax-qualified money into it without any tax penalty. You can keep the same set of tax laws and simply transfer the money into this new product and, in so doing, insure your retirement account against the damaging effects of a negative market. This solves the problem for those who have already accumulated most or all of their retirement money. It's the financial world's greatest gift to the retiree.

Before I share specifically how this wonderful financial tool works, I want to address the topic of annuities in general. Much like life insurance, annuities have developed a bad name in some circles. Is this bad name deserved? Absolutely not. But much like life insurance, this bad name has been created by three things: one, an immense amount of misunderstanding; two, a small number of unethical sales people; and, three, the fact that most of the money in this country is controlled by stockbrokers and money managers who generally don't sell (or understand) annuities, so they throw them under the bus in order to promote something they do offer.

I'd like to give you the real story on annuities – the good and the bad, what they are, and what they are not, and then I want *you* to decide whether it is a good fit for your specific financial situation.

The first thing you need to know is that there are three different kinds of annuities.

1. **Fixed Annuities** – which are interest rate based
2. **Variable Annuities** – which are equity based
3. **Indexed Annuities** – a hybrid that shares some characteristics of the previous two

Even though the purpose of this chapter is to highlight the unique benefits of Indexed Annuities, I want to give a brief explanation of the other two so you have a cursory understanding of how each works.

Fixed Annuity

A Fixed Annuity is much like a Certificate of Deposit (CD) offered by a bank. It pays a fixed rate of interest, thus the name. And just like a CD, the return on a Fixed Annuity is very safe. However, because it is safe, it offers a low interest rate and, thus, a low potential for growth.

While CDs generally charge penalties for any withdrawal prior to the end of the chosen term, Fixed Annuities commonly allow an individual to withdraw up to 10 percent of the account value each year *without* penalty. This makes Fixed Annuities more liquid (accessible) than most Certificates of Deposit, which is a very significant feature.

Also, unlike CDs, whose gain is taxed every year, Fixed Annuities grow tax-deferred, meaning taxes are not due on the gain until the money is actually withdrawn. The benefit of delaying taxes is that an individual earns interest on three things instead of just two:

1. The original principal
2. The interest (growth)
3. The future taxes retained within the annuity

This third feature, earning interest on Uncle Sam's future taxes, is unique to products offering tax-deferral, which allows a Fixed Annuity to grow faster than a CD paying the same rate of interest.

Another valuable feature of a Fixed Annuity is that it is

an insurance product, which allows the owner the ability to name a specific beneficiary (a person or organization) who will receive this money upon his or her death. The advantage of the beneficiary designation is that the annuity proceeds get paid directly to the chosen beneficiary, avoiding all of the expense, hassle, and delay of probate. It bypasses court completely, enabling heirs to receive the money in days instead of months. This is a huge benefit that cannot be overstated.

The last benefit I'd like to highlight is the Guaranteed Income feature that Fixed Annuities offer. Most of the time an annuity is simply a bucket of money, just like any other financial account. However, annuities also allow individuals to choose an additional benefit that other types of financial instruments generally don't provide – the benefit of receiving a guaranteed stream of income for life. An income the owner *cannot* outlive.

Now before you get too excited about this feature, it does have its own set of drawbacks. To turn this money into a stream of lifetime income, the individual must surrender the entire bucket of money over to the insurance company, which then turns it into a series of guaranteed, periodic payments for either a set period of years, or for the life of the annuity owner.

So what's bad about that? A couple of things. First, once the money is turned into a series of periodic payments, the owner no longer has access to, or control of, the entire account value. He trades the bucket of money for the certainty of a lifetime income. This can be seen as good or bad, depending on the needs and desires of the client.

However, I do think this feature, called annuitization, is where a lot of the annuity's misunderstanding occurs. Many individuals, even some in the financial profession, think that clients *must* turn their entire account value into this on-going stream of income, giving up the access to and control of their entire pot of money. This is simply *not* the case. A client is never forced to choose this option. It is simply that – an option. It's an option that would only be chosen if the client felt this stream of income would be of greater benefit to him than keeping control of the entire bucket of money. But the fact remains, it's always the client's prerogative, and it's nice to have options.

Variable Annuity

I'm going to keep this description relatively brief, since Variable Annuities share many of the same features as Fixed Annuities:

1. They generally allow a withdrawal up to 10 percent of the account value per year without penalty.
2. They provide tax-deferred growth, meaning taxes are not paid until money is withdrawn.
3. The benefit pays directly to the beneficiaries, bypassing probate completely.
4. And they also allow the owner the ability to choose a lifetime stream of guaranteed income, one that cannot be outlived.

But there are also some key differences.

The most significant difference between the two is risk. While a Fixed Annuity can be thought of much like a CD, a Variable Annuity can be thought of much like a mutual fund. To be clear, it is *not* a mutual fund, but the engine for growth is much the same, based largely (if not solely) on equities. While this can be of benefit to the owner in a rising market, it can be disastrous in a declining market. Variable Annuities can lose money, sometimes a lot of money. In a Variable Annuity, *the client generally bears 100 percent of the market risk* upon his or her shoulders.

So why would someone take this increased risk? Purely for the *hope* of a higher return. A return that might possibly combat the wiles of that dreaded villain, Mr. Inflation.

However, for those currently retired, taking that risk can have disastrous results. Just look at 2008.

The second area in which a Variable Annuity differs from a Fixed Annuity is the cost incurred by the owner. Since Variable Annuities are equity based, they usually incur management fees and charges that Fixed Annuities do not. While these fees can be outweighed by years of solid market growth, they can feel like a sucker-punch to the midsection in years of market decline. (As a side note, though, this is really no different than any other equity-based product. They all have fees and expenses that are charged regardless of whether the market is up or down.)

Indexed Annuity

Writing this chapter feels a little bit like the story of *Goldilocks and the Three Bears*. Remember the story? One porridge was *too* hot. One porridge was *too* cold. But one porridge was *just* right.

Such is the case in the annuity world. One annuity is safe but offers weak growth. One annuity offers growth *potential*, but is too risky for the retiree. But one annuity is just right. The Indexed Annuity. It provides both safety *and* an opportunity for solid growth. The Indexed Annuity takes positive features from both of its predecessors and blends them into a new and powerful product.

Just like Fixed and Variable Annuities, the Indexed Annuity offers the same four features discussed under the Variable Annuity: penalty-free withdrawal, tax-deferred growth, bypass of probate, and the option for a guaranteed lifetime income. Where it differs is that it provides:

- 100-percent safety against stock market declines ***and***
- Solid growth potential

Think about that for a moment. This is not a rhetorical question. Seriously, pause for a moment and ask yourself, *Where can I get the potential for an inflation-beating return and have 100-percent safety against market risk of not only my principal, but also of all my previous years of gains?*

If you can name another product that offers both of those things, then you are incredibly intelligent and industrious, because I can't find anything like it, and trust me, I've tried. It's unique.

I am convinced that many of the clients who purchased Indexed Annuities prior to 2008 didn't completely believe their agent when he or she told them that they would never lose money due to a stock market decline. Why do I think this? It's human nature. I'm sure most of the clients trusted them on one level, but on another level they were thinking, "Yeah, I've heard that before. I'll believe it when I see it."

Well, 2008 gave them the perfect opportunity for a white-knuckled test-drive. And guess what? It passed with flying colors. Indexed Annuities did just as the agent had promised. Even when the S&P 500 was down nearly 52 percent, the owners of Indexed Annuities didn't lose a penny. Not one. And not only did they not *lose* any money, but all their previous years of gains were protected as well. They kept it all. And once the market began to climb again, these Indexed Annuities began growing from their currently locked-in highs, making new gains, while other accounts were clawing back losses, scrambling to simply get back to even. That really is a retirement miracle!

So if you are currently retired, or have already accumulated most of your retirement dollars inside a tax-qualified account, you may be asking yourself, "What should I do?" As you would imagine, it is impossible to address every specific situation in the context of this chapter, but I will give you the same advice I proffered earlier in this book – it's *critical* that you meet with an honest and qualified financial professional who can evaluate your specific and individual needs and who can recommend the right solution for *you*.

Along that same line, it is also important for you to know that purchasing an annuity from a financial professional will generally *not* cost you more. Sure, the financial professional will receive compensation for selling you this product, but an annuity's commission does not get paid from the owner's deposit, but, rather, it is paid to the agent directly from the issuing life insurance company.

As a matter of fact, unlike other investment options, it is common for many annuities to actually pay a deposit *bonus* when they are purchased. Yes, a bonus. For instance, if an annuity paid a hypothetical 4-percent bonus, then the purchaser of this annuity would *make* $4,000 immediately for every $100,000 put into the annuity, giving his account a positive growth from day one.

So, if you are a retiree who has money in any tax-deferred plan, and you like the prospect of growing your account with zero market risk, then look no further. You've found your new home, and the sign hanging just inside the door reads, "Annuity sweet annuity."

Chapter 17

What Next?

In my first book, I mention briefly an individual named Charles Blondin. Now I want to tell you more of his story.

Charles Blondin was a Frenchman who lived from 1824 to 1897. He started training to be an acrobat at age 5, and by 6 he was already performing under the stage name "The Little Wonder." In his 20s he was one of the most popular performers in Europe, but his crowning achievement came in 1859 when he traveled to the United States and became the first person to cross the 160-foot-high gorge beneath Niagara Falls on a tightrope.[13] History reports that he walked back and forth across that span many times in various and amazing ways.

One time, in the most bizarre crossing of all, Blondin stopped halfway across the falls, sat down on the tightrope, and cooked and dined on an omelet high above the churning water below. Imagine that!

Another time, he convinced his manager to get on his back, and they journeyed back and forth across the rope together. They almost didn't make it. Yeah, go figure.

Charles Blondin, carrying his manager over Niagara Falls
(copyright expired)

As the story goes, one time he also pushed a wheelbarrow back and forth across the rope, high atop the crashing falls. And as he approached the side of the falls where he began, there was a crowd gathered to watch his miraculous feat.

As he neared the crowd, he yelled out for all to hear, "How many of you believe I can push this wheelbarrow across Niagara Falls?"

In unison, the crowd shouted their affirmation as they raised their hands skyward. They knew he could do it. They had just witnessed it.

So as the crowd quieted down, Mr. Blondin pointed to a young man in the front row, with his hand raised high, and said, "Then sir, I'd like you to get into my wheelbarrow."

Now the story doesn't say what happened next, but I'll tell you what I would have done. I would have quickly lowered my hand, wiped the excitement off my face, and scurried back through the crowd as fast as my legs would carry me, far, far away from that wheelbarrow and Mr. Blondin's invitation.

But wait. I *did* believe he could do it. I had just raised my hand in confirmation. Why wouldn't I be willing to climb in?

It's simple. There is an enormous disparity between believing something with our head and believing it through our actions. And how does this apply to you and to this book? Even if you intellectually believe everything I have outlined, simply *believing* it will make no tangible difference in your life. The important question is, "Are you going to believe it through action?" In other words, are you going to get into the wheelbarrow? What does that mean? How do you climb into the wheelbarrow?

In this case, getting into the wheelbarrow might mean setting aside any preconceived ideas you may have had up to this point. It might mean making an appointment to get together with a professional who can properly evaluate your specific situation. But most certainly it means that you check these concepts out for yourself, do your own investigation. Don't let the ignorance and opinions of others scare you away from what could be one of the most powerful financial tools you have ever encountered.

Be a person who thinks for him or herself. Do your own homework. Make your decisions based on fact, not simply the opinions of the masses – which are usually wrong, by the way. And for what it's worth, don't just take my word for it either. I really want you to give this concept a fair look, check out the facts, run the numbers, and then decide if this is the right fit – *for you.*

It is my hope that this book will breathe new life into your financial future, change the way you think about money, take away the fear of higher taxation in the future, and show you that you *can* succeed. But ultimately this is all up to you. *You* hold the key to your own financial future. The answer is waiting – but only for those who take action.

Appendix

Figure A

(Top marginal income tax rates, year by year, and the income level they apply to.)

Tax Year	Top Marginal tax rate (%)	Top Marginal tax rate (%) on earned income, if different <1>	Taxable income over
1913	7		500,000
1914	7		500,000
1915	7		500,000
1916	15		2,000,000
1917	67		2,000,000
1918	77		1,000,000
1919	73		1,000,000
1920	73		1,000,000
1921	73		1,000,000
1922	58		200,000
1923	43.5		200,000
1924	46		500,000

1925	25		100,000
1926	25		100,000
1927	25		100,000
1928	25		100,000
1929	24		100,000
1930	25		100,000
1931	25		100,000
1932	63		1,000,000
1933	63		1,000,000
1934	63		1,000,000
1935	63		1,000,000
1936	79		5,000,000
1937	79		5,000,000
1938	79		5,000,000
1939	79		5,000,000
1940	81.1		5,000,000
1941	81		5,000,000
1942	88		200,000
1943	88		200,000
1944	94 <2>		200,000
1945	94 <2>		200,000
1946	86.45 <3>		200,000
1947	86.45 <3>		200,000
1948	82.13 <4>		400,000
1949	82.13 <4>		400,000
1950	84.36		400,000
1951	91 <5>		400,000
1952	92 <6>		400,000

1953	92 <6>		400,000
1954	91 <7>		400,000
1955	91 <7>		400,000
1956	91 <7>		400,000
1957	91 <7>		400,000
1958	91 <7>		400,000
1959	91 <7>		400,000
1960	91 <7>		400,000
1961	91 <7>		400,000
1962	91 <7>		400,000
1963	91 <7>		400,000
1964	77		400,000
1965	70		200,000
1966	70		200,000
1967	70		200,000
1968	75.25		200,000
1969	77		200,000
1970	71.75		200,000
1971	70	60	200,000
1972	70	50	200,000
1973	70	50	200,000
1974	70	50	200,000
1975	70	50	200,000
1976	70	50	200,000
1977	70	50	203,200
1978	70	50	203,200
1979	70	50	215,400
1980	70	50	215,400

1981	69.125	50	215,400
1982	50		85,600
1983	50		109,400
1984	50		162,400
1985	50		169,020
1986	50		175,250
1987	38.5		90,000
1988	28 <8>		29,750 <8>
1989	28 <8>		30,950 <8>
1990	28 <8>		32,450 <8>
1991	31		82,150
1992	31		86,500
1993	39.6		89,150
1994	39.6		250,000
1995	39.6		256,500
1996	39.6		263,750
1997	39.6		271,050
1998	39.6		278,450
1999	39.6		283,150
2000	39.6		288,350
2001	39.1		297,350
2002	38.6		307,050
2003-2011	35		311,950-379,150

< 1 > This figure is cited when the top marginal rate for earned income differs from that for unearned income.

< 2 > For 1944-1945, the highest tax rate was subject to a maximum effective rate limitation equal to 90 percent of statutory "net income."

< 3 > For 1946-1947, the highest rate was subject to a maximum effective rate limitation equal to 85.5 percent of statutory "net income."

< 4 > For 1948-1949, the highest rate was subject to a maximum effective rate limitation equal to 77 percent of statutory "net income."

< 5 > For 1951, the highest rate was subject to a maximum effective rate limitation equal to 87.2 percent of statutory "net income."

< 6 > For 1952-1953, the highest rate was subject to a maximum effective rate limitation equal to 88 percent of statutory "net income."

< 7 > For 1954-1963, the highest rate was subject to a maximum effective rate limitation equal to 87 percent of statutory "net income."

< 8 > For 1988-1990, some taxpayers faced a 33-percent marginal tax rate in an income bracket above the one cited for the 28-percent rate. However, the marginal rate returned to 28 percent above this 33-percent bracket. That is, for all sufficiently high incomes, 28 percent was the marginal rate.[14]

Endnotes

1 USA Today, "Bill for Tax-Payers Swells by Trillions," by Dennis Cauchon, May 19, 2008.
2 www.truthinaccounting.org
3 http://www.usdebtclock.org
4 Comeback America: Turning the ... David Walker, 2009 ...
5 www.truthinaccounting.org
6 chart presentation linked to on truthin2010
7 "Obama Proposes $3.8 Trillion Budget on Jobs." By Roger Runningen and Brian Faler. February 1, 2010. Bloomberg.com
8 Wikipedia – Nikkei 225
9 Wikipedia – Dot-Com Bubble: http://en.wikipedia.org/wiki/Dot-com_bubble
10 MoneyChimp.com: *http://www.moneychimp.com/features/market_cagr.htm* – based on year end data through 2009.
11 MoneyChimp.com: *http://www.moneychimp.com/features/market_cagr.htm* – based on year end data through 2009.
12 http://truthandpolitics.org/top-rates.php
13 http://www.toptenz.net/top-10-daredevils.php
14 http://truthandpolitics.org/top-rates.php